Books by Katharine Scherman

Spring on an Arctic Island
The Long White Night
The Sword of Siegfried
William Tell
Catherine the Great
The Slave Who Freed Haiti:
The Story of Toussaint Louverture
Two Islands: Grand Manan and Sanibel

Two Islands

Grand Manan
and Sanibel

Two Islands

Grand Manan and Sanibel

by Katharine Scherman

Illustrated with photographs by the author

Little, Brown and Company—Boston—Toronto

LIBRARY OF CONGRESS CATALOG CARD NO. 78–143710

FIRST EDITION

T06/71

Published simultaneously in Canada
by Little, Brown & Company (Canada) Limited

PRINTED IN THE UNITED STATES OF AMERICA

For Axel

Contents

Illustrations

Two Islands

Introduction

$\mathcal{T}$wo islands, one north, one south, present a contrast irresistible to anyone fascinated by islands. Grand Manan is in the Bay of Fundy, lapped by the cold waters and fogs of the Labrador Current. Sanibel, off the Gulf coast of southern Florida, benefits from another current, the Gulf Stream. Both are temperate, both about the same size, large enough for weeks of exploring but not unmanageably big. In all other aspects they are entirely different.

Sanibel rose from the sea when Grand Manan was already

old. The southern island is still rising slowly, the northern one sinking. Nowhere over fourteen feet high, Sanibel is caressed by sun and wind most of the year, and always habitable. Grand Manan is cold and foggy and girt with crumbling cliffs, an island so grim and stormy at first appearance that no one dared live there until the late eighteenth century, when streams of New England Loyalists fled the American Revolution and overflowed from New Brunswick to the empty islands of the Bay of Fundy.

Islands are attractive to anyone who wants, for a short time, a feeling of escape. To be surrounded by water is to be in one's own castle, apart from everyday fears and hates. Many islands support their own specialized plant and animal life, distinct from the mainland. Their human inhabitants are liable also to be so out of touch with the rest of the world that visitors seem to them alien. The people of Grand Manan refer to their nearest countrymen on the mainland of New Brunswick as "foreigners."

Sanibel is closer to its mainland, and its few hundred year-round residents, for the most part, look forward to winter and early spring, and the tourists who come as inevitably as the hordes of migrant sandpipers. This gentle southern island has not had a happy history. First came the Spanish Conquistadores, to enslave, kill or drive away the Caloosa Indians, who were far more civilized than their invaders. Its subsequent intruders, up to the recent drug runners, have nearly always been riffraff seeking a concealed landfall. Only for forty-three years, from 1883 to 1926, did the island have a population of farmers, whose new homes restored a semblance of the Caloosas' garden retreats.

Grand Manan's story is one of struggle and hard work, fishing and farming, from the time of the first settlers to the present. Tourists are tolerated but not catered to, and the few small hotels, originally private houses, can accommodate a minimum of summer visitors. They are all closed in winter, their owners back in Toronto, or whatever mainland town they came from, to catch up with the world again.

My husband and I have visited Sanibel often enough to locate hidden eagles' nests, traverse by canoe the little-known lakes among the mangroves of the interior, walk an overgrown path lined with butterfly orchids. On Grand Manan there is weir fishing in the cold bright sunset, dark dank forests whose floors are covered with strange mushrooms, and the tall western cliff where no one goes except by mistake. We have been entranced by the essential remoteness of both islands.

The following pages are a record of an outsider's view. The residents know a great deal more, but generally they don't remark on it. Their own gardens or beach fronts or fishing boats engross them.

Nevertheless the people who live on Grand Manan and on Sanibel introduced us to small parts of their islands, their own private Edens. Without them this book could not have been written. I am deeply grateful.

Island in the Sea

Grand Manan

I.

*G*rand Manan is an awesome island, high-cliffed and thickly wooded. It stands solid, fifteen and a half miles long, six and a half miles at its widest, at the mouth of the Bay of Fundy, its southern tip pointed toward the Atlantic Ocean. Though forbidding at a distance it seems, near at hand, a fine place to live. It is surrounded by the cold waters of the Labrador Current, beloved of herring, cod and lobster. Nourished by the fogs of the great bay, its meadows are bright with green grass and field flowers and wild strawberries. Its forests

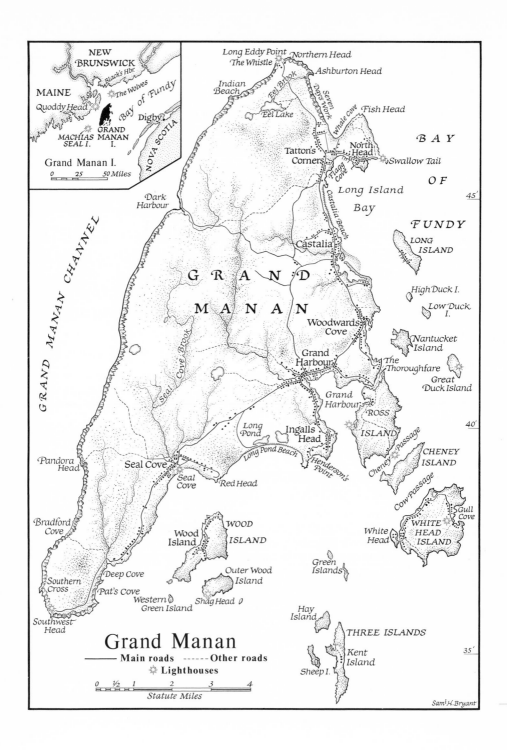

NEW
BRUNSWICK

Black's Hbr.

MAINE

The Wolves

Bay of Fundy

Quoddy Head

Digby?

GRAND MANAN I.

MACHIAS SEAL I.

NOVA SCOTIA

Grand Manan I.

0   25   50 Miles

Long Eddy Point   Northern Head
The Whistle   Ashburton Head

Indian Beach

Eel Brook

Eel Lake

Seven Days Work

Whale Cove

Fish Head

BAY

Tatton's Corners   North Head

Flagg Cove

Swallow Tail

OF

Long Island Bay

Castalia Beach

FUNDY

LONG ISLAND

Dark Harbour

GRAND MANAN CHANNEL

Castalia

G R A N D

M A N A N

High Duck I.

Low Duck I.

Woodwards Cove

Nantucket Island

Seal Cove Brook

Grand Harbour

The Thoroughfare

Great Duck Island

Grand Harbour

ROSS ISLAND

Pandora Head

Long Pond

Ingalls Head

Cheney Passage

CHENEY ISLAND

Seal Cove

Long Pond Beach

Henderson's Point

Seal Cove

Red Head

Cow Passage

WHITE HEAD ISLAND

Gull Cove

White Head

Bradford Cove

Wood Island

WOOD ISLAND

Outer Wood Island

Green Islands

Southern Cross

Deep Cove

Pat's Cove

Western Green Island

Shag Head

Hay Island

THREE ISLANDS

Southwest Head

Kent Island

Sheep I.

Grand Manan
—— Main roads ------ Other roads
✳ Lighthouses

0   ½   1   2   3   4
Statute Miles

Sam! H. Bryant

45'

40'

35'

of spruce, balsam, birch and poplar are underlaid with a heavy growth of fern and alder. There are no slums or shantytowns, and its small settlements of clean frame houses are surrounded by garden flowers, many of which have escaped to line the roads and lanes.

Lighthouses, bell buoys and foghorns continuously warn the sailor of reefs hidden by the twenty- to twenty-five-foot tide. Churches, sprinkled liberally through the villages, warn the holy and the unholy against the evils of whiskey and tobacco. It seems indeed a proper, safe and moderately comfortable island. Many of its twenty-seven hundred inhabitants are sturdy puritan descendants of Massachusetts Loyalists who fled the American Revolution, to fish the rich bay and till the fertile ground and cut the forest trees for masts and building. They do not want to live anywhere else.

It was not always so. Until 1784 this beautiful and potentially wealthy island was uninhabited. In fact it was feared and shunned. Its rocky coast, high tides and fierce currents are extremely dangerous to boats. The weather is often disagreeable. In summer there is fog, in winter strong winds, and rain is frequent all year round. It did not seem an island paradise to those who touched on it in the course of more fruitful explorations. Though there was a good-sized population of Indians in nearby Maine and southern Canada, none of them ever lived on Grand Manan. They visited it occasionally to collect the feathers and eggs of gull, tern and eider, but they did not stay. Even their name for it is inconsequential. Manan is a French-English corruption of *muna-nouk,* the local Indian word for "island in the sea" (as distinguished from lake island, river island, or hill island — Manhattan) and applied to a number of islands off the North Atlantic coast. "Grand" was supplied at a later date by the explorer Champlain.

Grand Manan was known to adventurous fishermen of Scandinavia, Brittany and Portugal who, though they were wary of landing, found an extraordinary abundance of fish off its shores. John Cabot sighted it in 1498 and Gaspar Cortoreal in 1501. A Portuguese map, published in 1558, shows a cape at the mouth of the bay called *C. de las muchas islas* (Cape of many islands), which included Grand Manan.

The first explorers to write of the known but yet uninhabited island were Pierre du Guast, sieur de Monts, and Samuel de Champlain, in 1606. They sailed, of necessity without charts, not knowing whether they would find harbors or reefs. Their ships, like most exploring vessels of the time, were designed for long trips and heavy seas. In coastal waters they were cumbrous and unwieldy. Not surprisingly Champlain viewed the island with dismay. The explorers sailed its length to measure it, the monstrous cliffs of the west coast leaning outward toward them. No break in the sheer rock afforded them shelter. Dark Harbour, the only cove on the west, was then entirely closed from the sea by a high dike of large pebbles washed down from the stony heights and reinforced by the mighty vigor of the outside water. Finally they halted and, as Champlain wrote in his journal, "passed a dreary night in a storm off Southern Head." It is not a friendly coast for ships, and Southwest Head is perhaps its least inviting stretch: a cliff two hundred feet high juts out into the sea, eddies curl at its base, and the tide climbs with alarming rapidity, engulfing first shoals, then pinnacles of rock. There is no sanctuary there. Ships today still pass well to the south of it, warned off by a lighthouse and a very noisy foghorn.

In 1613 the Jesuits, represented by Father Pierre Biard and Father Ennemonde Massé, made their first, and unpopular, attempt to establish a missionary post in New France. The Fathers were sent hither and yon along the coasts of what are now Maine, New Brunswick and Nova Scotia. On one of their hapless voyages in that region they were caught by a storm in the shadow of Grand Manan, as one of the Fathers noted in his journal, "and there came upon the sea such a dense fog that we could see no more by day than by night. . . . In this place there are breakers and rocks, against which we were afraid of striking in the darkness; the wind not permitting us to draw away and stand out to sea." When the Fathers were finally forced to find a ship to take them back to France they once more stumbled against the difficult island. The journal continues: "A very angry sea caused by the strong violent currents . . . kept [us] there eight or nine days." They had recourse to prayers for the mercy of God, and were saved to reach their homeland at last.

Among their harassments were the maneuvers of a Virginian, Captain Samuel Argall, who not only stole their commission and declared them trespassers on English territory, but denounced the unfortunate missionaries as outlaws and pirates who should be hanged. He had been sent with three ships to destroy the French settlements in Acadia (the Maritime Provinces). He destroyed nothing on Grand Manan because there was no one there, but the island, along with most of the mainland, became temporarily British.

For the next 146 years Grand Manan was tossed back and forth between France and England, depending on who came out the loser in the depressingly frequent wars of the seventeenth and eighteenth centuries. Bands of marauders made all the islands and boundaries of Acadia unattractive to settlers, and Grand Manan was avoided even more resolutely than before. In 1621, during a British period, the island was granted by James I, as part of New Brunswick and Nova Scotia, to Sir William Alexander. But Grand Manan, a stepchild, was cut in half, the southwest part being outside the

*Below Southwest Head light guil-
lemots nest on the cliff. Southward,
toward the Atlantic, are the reefs
that plagued Champlain when he
tried to anchor in 1606.*

boundary. There was no one to care. Shortly afterward it was French again, and in 1693 was presented by Count Frontenac, governor of New France, to Paul Dailleboust, sieur de Perigny, a knight who had fought well against the English in Acadia. He was to enjoy all the privileges of hunting, fishing and trade with the Indians; also to mark oak trees suitable for shipbuilding and to keep an eye out for minerals. The grant was attractive — think of being *given* Grand Manan — but the courageous warrior, apparently preferring battle to the green foggy peace of a lonely island, never set foot on it or sent any settlers there. His grant lapsed to the crown.

After the fall of Quebec to the British in 1759 Acadia became finally and firmly a British colony. There was to be no more anarchy. Despite the peace and the consequent settlement of the mainland, Grand Manan, only a few miles off the coast, remained a wilderness, hardly mentioned in the records. An English voyager, Captain William Owen, described its attractions and disadvantages in his account of a visit there in 1770. First landfall was a salt marsh on the east coast near what is now the village of Castalia. He found it an indifferent harbor which, however, might in a crisis "serve as a tolerable asylum for fishermen and small craft." His main diversion was shooting black ducks; the marsh was a haven for ducks and shorebirds in those days before the herring gulls took over. Leaving the marsh he sailed southward, but the next anchorage was dismal. He entered a channel that seemed safe and deep, the calm inner passage between Ross and Cheney Islands, which are sprigs of the main island, though Captain Owen could not know this. The tide receded, and in a remarkably short time the boat was entirely out of water. He and his crew crossed the mud on foot to Grand Manan, where an Indian offered them shelter. They amused themselves, as before, shooting birds — mergansers and loons. In due time the boat was adrift again but, Owen wrote, "it was with great difficulty we got through with our sails and oars; for the first quarter flood runs here with great rapidity." It is, in fact, four knots or more. The next stop was Grand Harbour, where a group of Englishmen were cutting and drying hay. The Englishmen, he found, did not live on the island, nor did the Indians. The meadow grass was rich and the timber abundant, but they all preferred the mainland for their houses and stock. The English boat, called the *Hay Sloop,* was anchored nearby, and the guard gave him some fine lobsters. At first look Grand Harbour was a magnificent anchorage, deep and sheltered, but Captain Owen evidently took a second look, because he "would not recommend it to Vessels of burthen, unless in stress of weather, or real business." The second look must have been near low tide, when the splendid expanse of water is flushed out as if by a pump, leaving a vast acreage of mud, rocks and seaweed. Captain Owen's last stop was Seal Cove, about which he was somewhat more enthusiastic, probably because he did not see it at low tide. In fact he left as soon as possible, pursued by gales and fogs and convinced, as had been adventurers before him, that Grand Manan, for all its ducks and lobsters, was a place neither to visit nor to live.

When the American Revolution broke out, streams of Loyalists, eventually numbering about forty thousand, fled to the relative safety of English Canada, probably planning to return to their comfortable New England farms once the British soldiers had subdued the foolhardy insurgents. In 1779 three families actually went to Grand Manan for peace and shelter. They built huts and lived a precarious existence, harassed by pirates from Machias. Machias, now a small quiet town near the coast of Maine, had set itself up as a province independent of both governments, and its citizens set on Revolutionaries and Loyalists alike with guerrilla warfare and piracy. Their fierceness cowed both soldier (usually more attached to his farm than his musket) and unarmed settler.

The newcomers on Grand Manan had to contend not only with the reign of terror from the mainland but the venality of the Indians. The latter, who had never lived on the island and had no claim to it, demanded payment from the few settlers for the right to remain there unmolested. Grand Manan was thus "sold" to the colonists for ten dollars and a heifer. It is not clear whether this was a fair price, considering Grand Manan's unpopularity. It was, however, cheaper than Manhattan, not counting the heifer, and a fraction of the price of a barrel of rum. Rum was a big item in the province of New Brunswick, of which Grand Manan was part. The smaller fish, mostly herring, caught by torchlight, were salted and smoked and shipped to the West Indies; there exchanged for more salt, a plentiful commodity in the Caribbean, and as much rum as the holds would carry. In the course of one year, 1787–1788, New Brunswick imported rum to the amount of four gallons for every man, woman and child.

But even peace, possession, rum and herring couldn't keep the settlers there. They departed after a year, with the distinction only of producing the first white child born on the island, one Alexander Bonny, whose father's name now adorns a small river on the eastern coast.

At the end of the Revolution, in 1783, more refugees flooded the Maritimes, and license was granted by the New Brunswick government to fifty families "to Occupy during pleasure the Island of Grand Manan and the small Islands adjacent in the Fishery, with Liberty of Cutting Flake Stuff [wood for making fish-drying racks, called flakes] and Timber for Building Hutts and Stores, and Wood for firing."

It seemed that at last the island's wealth of fish and lumber was to be exploited, and its "rude and magnificent scenes" described by a temporary visitor, appreciated. But the living was too hard for most of the new settlers, who returned to the mainland after less than a year of storms and fogs. A report in 1786, while lauding the timber and the excellent soil, describes the island as entirely destitute of inhabitants. This was not quite true. A few hardy families remained, and their descendants are still there.

But trouble pursued them. Grand Manan's hidden coves enticed American privateers during the War of 1812. The new inhabitants, now firmly attached to their land, defied the marauders with spirit. A band of pirates sailed into Grand Harbour with the intention of stealing a schooner. It was obvious what they were about, and before they could get near the prize its owner quickly removed a plank from the bottom and left the schooner to the thieves. Unable to mend it, they left the harbor. Another party demanded potatoes from a farmer at Seal Cove, who haughtily refused, but added, pointing to the field : "There are the potatoes, and if you are rascals enough to steal them you must dig them." The rascals departed. They were, in fact, far less efficient and dedicated than the raging crews from Machias in the hot days of the Revolution. The colonists tended to laugh at them, and their boats were run aground or chased out of the harbors by British cruisers. Everyone except the pirates found the routs exciting. The pirate craft had bold names, *Weazel, Revenge, Growler, Wasp,* but their crews were more raffish than fierce, and many of the vessels were only open rowboats.

After the War of 1812 there was intermittent haggling between Great Britain and the United States over the ownership of Grand Manan. In 1817 it was declared formally to be within the bounds of New Brunswick, Canada. However, some United States families had settled there after the Loyalist influx had died down, and no one seemed to know whether the island's sympathies lay with republican New England or a distant monarch in Old England. John Dunn, then sheriff of the county of Charlotte, which includes Grand Manan, wrote of its inhabitants in a report to his government: "We will never be able to make these fellows *good* British subjects." As late as 1841 there was still dissension, and Daniel Webster wrote: "We think that Grand Menan [the old French spelling] should have been assigned to us." Not until 1842 was the boundary between the United States and Canada settled beyond doubt.

When you look at a map you can see that Webster may have been right. The island is barely seven miles off the coast of Maine and eighteen miles from Blacks Harbour, the nearest shipping point in Canada. Its settlers were American-born, not English; its allegiances after the Treaty of Paris in 1783 were mixed. In the first half of the nineteenth century American fishermen were far more active around Grand Manan than the islanders themselves, not only because of their industry and expertise, but because the waters were richer in cod and herring than those off the New England coast. The islanders showed less animosity to the intruders from the south than toward the fishermen from Canada's mainland, known in Grand Manan as "foreigners."

The population of the island seemed to the worried mainland government a distinct class, apathetic and slothful. In 1834 the inhabitants numbered 956, scattered along the east coast without proper towns, schools or churches; poor fishermen-farmers, with only sixteen fishing boats (now there are 144 over ten tons, and a host of powered dories and rowboats for inshore fishing and dulse gathering). It has been estimated that in those days more than 1,000 barrels of herring, or 105,000 dry quarts, found their way into one brush weir in a single tide. But the owners took out only 100 barrels and opened the weir, allowing the others to escape. The Atlantic coast sardine industry had not yet developed, and the people considered the young herring not worth curing. If they chanced to take more small fish than they had use for, they left them to rot on the beach and wash back into the sea on the tide, where their decaying bodies spoiled the weirs. Or else — and this seemed a peculiarly offensive practice — they took the extra fish in wagon loads to the fields for manure. Whatever the wastrels on Grand Manan did with the young herring, the opinion on the mainland was that so many destroyed meant so many not caught and sold as adults. The herring, it was thought, were definitely going somewhere else to spawn, or there were not enough left to spawn at all. This was a matter of deep concern to those who wanted Grand Manan to take its just place as the finest fishery on the Atlantic coast. Today sardines are a delicacy, and millions of pounds of herring go into the production of fertilizer, yet the population does not appear to be declining.

While the mainland government considered Grand Mananers careless, lazy and insular, probably only the latter was true (and still is). For a hundred years after its settlement the island was not connected to the mainland by regular mail and passenger boat, and the pioneers had to be self-sufficient to live at all. They farmed and they fished, and for the most part they consumed what they produced. They cut slender young trees for brush weirs and others for masts, firewood and building, but there was no extensive lumbering. In fact, far removed from commerce, nothing was extensive on Grand Manan. It must have appeared an island of singular grace and peace to the traveler with courage to brave the tides, the offshore rocks and the currents.

It was not until 1884 that the first regular mail and passenger boat started operation between Grand Manan and the mainland. The little ship had begun life as a ferry between Flushing and New York, and was known simply as *Flushing*. The second boat was also from New York, an excursion boat called *Aurora*. The third was a steel ship nicknamed *The Iron Duke,* and made specially for the island route. The fourth had been originally a private yacht named *Elk,* supremely comfortable, even elegant. The last three were renamed in monotonous succession, *Grand Manan, Grand Manan II,* and *Grand Manan III*. Now there is a functional new ferry built at a cost of two million dollars by the Connors Sardine Company, which has plants on the island and mainland. It is called, again, *Grand Manan*.

It is comparatively easy now to get to the island, though still not easy enough to attract the casual tourist. You have to really want to go there. You drive a long winding road from the Maine border to Blacks Harbour, a utilitarian town devoted to the sardine industry as represented by Connors. You are greeted by the only road sign for miles, "Connors — the World's Largest Sardine Industry," and a strong smell of fish fertilizer. This plain village is far off train and bus lines. It has no hotel and no shops, and the ferry dock at the bottom of a rutted road on a muddy cape outside the town has nothing whatsoever to recommend it. A tourist coming on this cape by mistake — an almost impossible mistake since it is far from the main road, and not even marked on most maps — would wonder at the fat new boat tied to the raw new dock. A first-time visitor to Grand Manan would be inclined to turn back.

If he stays a sense of leisure takes over necessarily. The cars used to be hoisted from the dock to the hold in heavy net slings, one for each wheel. (Now there is a power-operated ramp to cope with the tide. Sometimes the ramp doesn't work, and the slings still travel with the boat.) The loading crew seems in no hurry. They joke with one another as the cars swing in open air, and the first mate, a fine, handsome, efficient man, unobtrusively turns his head away as fearful car owners approach him for assurance that their vehicles won't land in the bay. One has to relax. After the cars are loaded there comes a large miscellany of freight for the island, from building planks to hundreds of blue-frosted cakes for Father's Day in boxes with plastic cufflinks in their transparent windows. Finally the mail truck comes, taking up space that could be used for two more cars. There are usually more cars waiting than the boat can hold (twenty-three is its limit), so the smart traveler gets there the night before and locks his car in position. One day this trick misfired. The ferry was to make its return journey from its home port at Grand Manan. An islander drove his car onto the dock late at night and, feeling sleepy, climbed in the back seat, leaving the key in the ignition. He dropped off, watching the stars and thinking about life, or maybe the price of lobster. The first mate got down early the next morning, half asleep himself, drove the car into the slings and let the crew hoist it up. The owner of the car woke when he was hovering over the hold and gave a shout of alarm. The crew, of course, laughed.

The ride over the bay in the seaworthy 1443.29-ton boat takes a comfortable two hours. One can eat at a cafeteria or sit on an upholstered bench, trying to ignore the piped radio music and commercials, and looking out at white cotton. The fog of the Bay of Fundy is massive. Nothing can be seen, not even a gull. It is this frequent fog, combined with the rapid tide, that makes the bay dangerous for boats, even though it is protected from the worst storms of the outer Atlantic. Foghorns and bell buoys sound in all directions; on this short run one is obviously never far from islands, shoals and reefs. However the captain is serene. Long experience, aided by radar and radio, gives him confidence. He can land the bulky ship at the

North Head dock at Grand Manan even when the dock is invisible from twenty-five feet away.

Axel, my husband, and I debarked on the island's gentle east coast of fields, lagoons, flowers and small villages. We went to stay in one of a group of houses, among the oldest on the island, built in 1810. These little houses are still upright, comfortable and easy to heat. The walls and roofs are shingled, silver in the sun, dark brown in the rain. The chimneys are of old red brick and all the low-ceilinged rooms have fireplaces or wood-burning stoves. The furniture is simple and well proportioned and much of it is handmade. Though these houses and the few others like them that have not been allowed to deteriorate were built by people of little education and almost no contact with the rest of the world, they are not primitive. Excellent building and natural good taste make them far more livable than the rows of ugly prefabricated cottages put up for the sardine factory workers at the mainland end of the ferry run.

The site is as beautiful as the buildings. No doubt necessity directed its choice. At the bottom of a field strewn with creeping juniper and pasture is Whale Cove, a wide curve of pebble beach, ten minutes' walk from the dwellings, where the early fishermen-farmers kept their boats. Orchard, pasture and vegetable plots were behind the houses, keeping at bay the heavy forest (heavy no longer). The orchard is still there, untended, fenced with a line of tall spruces that the ubiquitous lumbermen were never allowed to touch. The pasture is there, too, part of it cut as a lawn between the houses, most allowed to grow wild. Columbine and garden lupine, pink, white and violet, have escaped to touch the long green grass with color, and lilac grows tall along the rutted driveway. A mockingbird perches on a post in the field and sings, quite at home, far from his usual southern haunts. Far in the

The oldest houses, built in 1810 by fishermen-farmers and still lived in, are shingled, with wood-burning stoves and small rooms to withstand the winter cold.

woods, at evening, flutelike voices of Swainson's thrushes echo one another in circling, rising notes. In the old spruces goldfinches trill, high and sweet, purple finches sing their melodic dreamy songs and red crossbills work busily among the cones, clicking as they fly from one tree to another. A pair of cedar waxwings, almost tame, have an untidy nest too far out on an apple tree branch in the orchard. Only four of the five bluish, black-spotted eggs have hatched, and two of the naked nestlings fell out when a strong wind shook one side of the nest from its flimsy mooring. The parents, unconcerned with the closeness of our doorstep, take turns feeding the young and carefully (in spite of their slovenly nest they are tender parents) protecting them from sun and rain. Though waxwings love fruit and berries in season, they also eat insects, darting like flycatchers. One parent found a cobweb in the tree and sat beside it — black-masked, crested and elegant — picking out the bugs one by one until they were all gone.

Sheep trails, now marked with red paint and uninhabited by sheep, lure the walker into tangles of alder and blackberry and fallen trees, relieved by uncluttered spaces of spruce and balsam and small meadows bright with wild flowers. From the trails that drift up and down along the high shore there are occasional glimpses of the Bay of Fundy far below, blue and gentle, and the kidney-shaped brush weirs that seem to have grown there.

Not all of the island is so beautiful; the despoilers of our century have been at it. But one can still find flowered fields and shadowed woods here and there, free of garbage and abandoned cars, and sphagnum bogs thick with exotic plant life, and unsullied beaches of dark basaltic sand. Wherever you are there is the sense of fog and ocean, and always a damp wind bringing the smell of seaweed. Also, in the summer, there are blackflies and mosquitoes, born of the same soft dampness that makes the fields so green and the flowers so vivid.

Grand Manan attracts few visitors and has little frivolity, organized or unorganized. The water is cold for swimming and dangerous for sailing. The fishermen go out to catch fish in a businesslike way, and the sport fisherman who wants to try his hand in the Bay of Fundy usually comes back with one halibut and a desperate case of seasickness. The small-boat fishermen are kind and will take out anyone who wants to go. But they have a living to make, and they warn the guest that they will come back only when they are ready, not when he is. The bay seldom looks rough, but there is a strong though invisible swell on its smooth surface, so the sportsman suffers while the islanders, inured, go on fishing.

The visitor is for the most part thrown back on himself and whatever pleasure he can derive from contemplating the island's proliferating wildlife and dramatic rock formations. Most of Grand Manan is relatively new, dating back to the Triassic period, some 200 million years ago, when volcanic eruptions created mountains and cliffs along the North Atlantic coast. But nine narrow miles of shoreline on Grand Manan's east coast are ancient, ranging from Paleozoic to Precambrian, 360 million to two billion years old. Long before the new rocks came violently out of the ocean the group of islands now called the Grand Manan Archipelago was a range of mountains rising from a river valley which is the present floor of the Bay of Fundy. These hills still have their heads above the sea, though they are sinking, worn by continuous though mild assault of water. Kent, White Head, Ross, Cheney and many other islands, some no more than smooth reefs visible at low tide, are the wave-subdued tops of the old range. Some are still connected with Grand Manan, and can be walked to at neap tide. The main island's short inhabited coast, long denuded and eroded by the sea, is low and deeply indented, and is sternly bounded by cliffs and mountains to the north, south and west.

2.

We started with the headland to the north of Whale Cove, where molten rock had slid over the old beaches, creating a 150-foot wall. It is called Seven Days' Work, not for its steepness but because on its face are seven rock layers, said to be seven strata of the earth's crust. We walked along the top of this cliff, occasionally skirting the edge, where once sheep had paused, not to view but to crop the grass that grew where trees could not find a foothold. An old-time resident, who helped maintain and map the trail, warned: "Do not get to the extreme edge, as there is real danger of the cliff giving way." However the red-marked trail now does hug the extreme edge: the cliff obviously has given way. Smooth alder has taken over the bare places, and there is a sheer drop to the water. Alder is deceptive, as it grows right over the edge. This species can reach a height of ten feet, but here it is hardly more than a ground cover, spreading thickly, its dense leaves masking the sudden fall of rock. We could not see the face of the cliff we were skirting, but after about a mile the land rises abruptly to the sharp rock of Ashburton Head, covered with grass and thrusting well out from the shore. A few wind-stunted spruces survive, but they do not obscure the headlong drop to the sea and the sweep of shoreline. Seven Days' Work is entirely exposed, a geometric arrangement of layers of rock like dark slate, a crystalline formation called schistose, from the Greek *schistos,* meaning split. It is astonishingly even in color and line, and sheer as a wall: it looks, as its name implies, like a gigantic work of architecture. Beyond it, in water only slightly darker blue than the sky, are the rounded brush weirs of Whale Cove, looking less artificial than the layered cliff. Farther south we can see the protuberance of Fish Head, one of the few bluffs that has resisted the slow force of the sea for many millions of years. It is a gentle, much eroded rise, and the history of the land lies before us. We stand on rock formed in one of the violent eruptions that obliterated Grand Manan's smoothed hills and slid at last, in semiliquid flow, down to Whale Cove, where the lava petered out, leaving bare a few miles of the old foundations that were probably part of the earth's first crust.

Ashburton Head itself is an intimidating rock. It looks inaccessible but at least once it was climbed. This was by one of the eight survivors of the ship *Lord Ashburton,* which was literally thrown against the shore while sailing off course in a nighttime winter storm in 1857. Twenty-one men were killed, but seven clung to pieces of the breaking hull and somehow were later rescued (no one now knows how), and the eighth actually crawled up the icy cliff, losing his boots and freezing his feet. We stared down the precipitate tumble of rock and wondered how he did it, but no doubt he took no time to wonder. Life was before him, death behind.

Many years later geologists analyzing Seven Days' Work and Ashburton Head came on sections of puzzling loose rock. There is plenty of loose rock lying around on Grand Manan, but it was odd to find some previously known only in the south of France. For a short time this was considered a geological first; then an islander casually mentioned the wreck of 1857. Some elementary research revealed that the loose rock *had* come from southern France. It was carried as ballast in the *Lord Ashburton,* which had sailed from Toulon to its fate on the cliff.

The trail between Ashburton Head and Whale Cove goes up and down in sharp little inclines, as do all Grand Manan's sheep tracks. In one of the valleys there was a low spruce branch under which a song sparrow had made a deep small nest, weaving it from the fine grass all around. Four fat eggs were in it, pale gray with reddish spots and stains. They were unevenly speckled, to melt into sun and shadow. It was a skillfully built nest, like a formation of the grass itself, and the spruce branch, sweeping the ground, protected it from rain, sun and straying gulls. It did not protect the eggs from something else, however, probably one of the many noisy, lively red squirrels of the spruce woods, to whom the little round eggs are a delicacy. We went back the day after we found it, and nothing was left but one shred of shell. The song sparrows did not return. Perhaps they made a new nest; perhaps it was a momentous tragedy. However we feel, the birds do not ex-

Ancient bluffs on the east coast, that have withstood the sea for millions of years, enclose small lonely beaches.

press obvious sorrow, and they all come back again the next year.

Near the nest is a turnoff downward to the sea. It is a scramble, slippery but not difficult, and at the bottom is a secluded beach, lonely, warm, sunny. This is the culmination of Eel Brook, which flows from the heights of the inland forest and buries itself under the pebbles of the upper beach, not visibly emptying into the sea. One has the sense that one cannot be reached here, surrounded as the cove is by tall promontories. There is no debris on this beach, as no road reaches it, and picnickers have to work to get here. There are a lot of large flat stones good for leaning against, and toward the water are the pervasive small cobbles of the island's beaches. The water is inviting on a good day, but its promise is false. I put a foot in it and it came out numb.

The Eel Brook Beach trail is obliterated in the other direction. But somewhere there was a falls, and one gray day we set out to find it, climbing with difficulty up the rough canyon cut through rock by the brook. We came on it unexpectedly. The canyon widened, and down two smooth slabs of rock came a rush of water. At the entrance to this open chamber in the forest grew one spiraled mushroom. The color was light brown, and the layers were delicately fringed with white. It was small, perfect, not more than an inch and a half high, and it was there only once. I have never seen one like it, and it may have been a growth stage of a familiar mushroom. The effect was odd: it seemed to have come when we did and to have evaporated when we left. We stepped carefully over it and entered a changed world. Ragged mist flew down through the treetops, obscuring the stream; the sky was suddenly almost black and absolute silence fell — except for the sibilance of the falls — all at once, the instant we stepped over the threshold. An earlier generation might have thought it a forbidden place of magic. To us the immediate effect was of a strange and unfriendly atmosphere, as if we were being told we had found the falls by mistake, and should leave it to itself, surrounded by its fence of almost impenetrable bramble and alder. The first heavy drops of rain came, and we fled from the wild, closed, mushroom-guarded spot. Later we went back, finding an easy trail from the road. The enchantment remained, but it was no more than that of a surprising and beautiful opening in the dense forest. The mushroom was not there.

Whale Cove is the beginning of the nine miles of old, relatively flat land, but you have to climb anyway for a while. The sheep trail rises from the beach and crawls through short spruces and massed alder along the top. Each year the trails are marked and partially cleared by a few regular summer visitors who like to walk; but on our spring visit the dedicated bushwhackers had not yet arrived, and last year's paint daubs were on rocks hidden by dense young fern, or on the trunks of trees toppled by the storms of the previous winter. It is impossible to get lost, however. We kept the sea on our left, waded through underbrush, branches snapping at our faces, and emerged, scathed, on an open field on a rock shelf.

We sat there in the sun for a while, enjoying the sea wind that never fails on that shore. Rising from the water was a great arch, called Hole in the Wall, through which the waves sucked and whispered, gently but inevitably undermining the headland, washing out the softer rock. The harder rock, hanging over emptiness, would fall in some winter storm. Above the arch, clusters of bluebells and daisies hung from rock crevices, like garlands on the bare cliff, and just above them, where sediment had collected in enough quantity to cover the terraced plateaus, were raspberry bushes, later to bear myriads of small, sweet berries.

35

*Swallow Tail light is on a
promontory almost severed
from the island by wave
action. The ferry whistles
in salute as it passes.*

Three bottle-nosed dolphins traveled and played close to shore. As they passed the point, we heard them breathe each time they arched in the air, a sound like a vast sigh. There was nothing dolorous about them, however. As do most sea mammals, they were expelling as much breath as possible in order to dive. Their bodies are encased in thick layers of fat, and if they did not let air out they would bounce back to the surface and float. This procedure seems strange to humans, who ordinarily inhale before going underwater, possibly because they would rather float than sink.

The trail goes on to Fish Head, a promontory named for its shape. The path winds, rising and dipping through the wind-stunted seaside forest, and finally ends at Swallow Tail lighthouse on a sweep of narrow headland covered by short grass, with a rocky tip thrusting out into the bay. This headland has become so eroded that it is almost separate from the island. A narrow bridge hangs over the water-filled canyon, called Saw Pit, and the lighthouse keepers have to walk across it to work.

In the thick woodland behind Swallow Tail we heard the songs of birds, but the singers were invisible. From a spruce came the fluid periods of a hermit thrush, each phrase higher than the last until the voice seemed to soar into a singer's Eden where human pitch was left behind and even human thought was earthbound. A Swainson's thrush in another tree defied us with deft, upward-spiraling song. A white-throated sparrow sang his few mournful quavering notes and a black-throated green warbler whispered his. It was the time of nesting, and the males were defending their property, but keeping out of sight. Possibly there were eggs, but there were not yet young, and the parents did not hover anxiously nearby as they would later. In a few weeks they would be trying to protect and appease irritable fledglings as they fluttered inefficiently from twig to twig, discounting danger and demanding food.

Now, in June, each tree and shrub had a song at its heart, and we listened, enthralled, without seeing so much as a leaf move.

At our feet, in the few spaces cleared of underbrush by larger spruces, were the small flowers that can exist only in the shade of northern forests. Bunchberry, or dwarf dogwood, had four showy white leaves that looked like petals surrounding clusters of small greenish flowers. Rounded and robust, it contrasted with the frail starflower, an attenuated primrose whose seven fine petals glowed in the half twilight. Once in a while there was a stretch of twinflower, a creeping plant of the honeysuckle family. Faint fragrance came from the paired pink blossoms, narrowly bell-shaped and pointed downward from erect stems. The twinflower likes moss and very deep shade. Carolus Linnaeus chose it as his name flower, *Linnaea borealis,* and it is recorded that he sometimes wore a twinflower in his buttonhole. I picked one and put it in my buttonhole, and in half an hour it was a pair of drooping dull pink threads. I could only think that the botanist, when he wore it, was not crawling on his stomach under fallen timber or negotiating a neck-high patch of blackberry bramble. All the flowers of the woods — there were not many — were small and existed on sufferance, protected by the few great trees still standing. Around them, outside the shade, were tangles of alder and bramble and bracken, the shrubs that come up readily after extensive timbering. They are excellent homes for birds and minor but irritating obstacles to human walkers. Perhaps that is the way it should be.

3.

*S*wallow Tail is the easternmost point of the cape of North Head, and the end of the ancient bluffs of the east coast. Southward the land is low, with harbors and tidal marshes and fields. On this short stretch of island are all the island's settlements but one. It is the civilized part of Grand Manan, with sardine canneries, vegetable gardens, cattle and, most common, the boats, nets and gear of the fishermen, who form the largest part of the male population.

There is also an extraordinary number of plain white

painted wood churches, mostly Baptist and well patronized. Some years ago a Baptist revivalist team arrived on the island full of missionary zeal. The inhabitants had been chiefly Anglican, but the then minister was not popular. The Baptists held a few hearty prayer meetings with exhortations, hymns and public confessions of sin, and won the wholehearted support of the islanders. Religion became almost their only entertainment — and remains so. Churches and sects multiplied; in one village there are two identical churches separated by a narrow driveway. One is named the Reformed Baptist Church; its brother (or enemy) the United Baptist Church, recently renamed the Wesleyan Methodist Church. Along with lively revival meetings the Baptists introduced a strong puritan morality. The sale of liquor was forbidden until recently. It used to travel abundantly on the ferry from the mainland, depriving Grand Manan of a good source of income. But for a year the island was virtually liquorless. Blacks Harbour, the new ferry terminus, has no government liquor store; in addition the island's one policeman came down hard on those who used to buy on the mainland and sell privately, for a small profit, on the North Head dock. Now Grand Manan has, against strong protest from the churches, a package store. We were inclined to think it a good thing until we went down to the dock one Saturday evening, when all the boats of the fishing fleet were in, and every other man there was reeling. They managed somehow to get out to sea on Sunday afternoon but there were a lot of bleary eyes and unshaven chins.

Tobacco is still hard to come by. If one asks for cigarettes there is a chilly denial. We were introduced to one sinner who sold cigarettes. He is well patronized. I asked in a general store for lipstick. "He don't stock lipstick," said the clerk, sounding as if I had asked for heroin. However, somehow, people smoke and paint their faces. Grand Manan is not a monastery, however much the Baptists would like to have it so.

There are some other peculiarities. I had a pair of excellent mountain-climbing boots which started to come apart at the soles, from age. But there is no shoemaker. I took them, on advice, to the man who makes wooden seagulls and fastens them on small pieces of driftwood. He said my shoes were too good for him to ruin. What happens, I asked, when the fishermen's shoes are damaged? They throw them away and get new ones, he said; an odd bit of extravagance. However, there is a truly excellent watch repairman, a doctor, a dentist who comes for a few weeks in the summer, and a hospital which was someone's large, old-fashioned family house. The hospital gets its patients, as soon as they are able to travel, off on the ferry to the St. John or St. Andrews hospitals. These are the extent of Grand Manan's services.

Even twenty-seven hundred people, with their churches and their fish factories, do not crowd the east coast (the population has been on a slow increase since 1881, when for the first time the number went over two thousand).

The oldest houses are brown-shingled, built by early settlers. There are not many left. They were too small for growing families, and most have been deserted, and have deteriorated. A few, like those at Whale Cove, are cherished and more beautiful than anything built since. Later houses were built of solid frame, white painted. They are not elegant or even interesting, but they are well cared for and ample. The newest come in pastel shades, and add color if not architectural beauty. Grand Manan is the wealthiest section of New Brunswick, and its large, clean, well-spaced houses attest to its superior respectability. There are many colorful gardens, as flowers grow for the asking in the fertile, damp earth. Among the lupine, roses and Canterbury bells in the front yards are numerous toys, tricycles, bicycles and a number of Hondas. The island is contributing its bit to the general world population increase, and large numbers of remarkably beautiful flaxen-haired little children play dangerously in the middle of the one main road, while their older motorized brothers roar in close circles in the driveways, on and off the highway and even on neighbors' front lawns.

Most of the houses are gathered in the five villages, and as soon as you leave them behind, the twentieth century seems to slip away. You know you are still in it, however, when you come to a lonely beach or an empty field and see a heap of garbage or a wheelless, rusted car. Much garbage these days is indestructible, and the white plastic bottles that litter the shores will exist far longer than we. The edible garbage attracts rats, and when the tide washes it out it sticks in the brush weirs and poisons the herring. Grand Manan has no adequate facilities for garbage disposal, though it has two open, evil-smelling pits. Generally the people strew their waste wherever it is convenient. So you have to get away not only from the towns but from the smell and ugliness of the dumps. This is easy. No one is going to carry garbage far from his car, so you leave the road. A few yards from it you are really on virgin land.

We walked long on beaches, on the edges of coastal swamps, through bogs, around lakes, without meeting anyone and without seeing one plastic bottle or orange peel. There was a big field just back of a beach, uncut and so brilliant with flowers that the eyes could not leave it: hawkweed, orange and yellow, purple clover, bluebells, daisies, wild lupine, sky-bright blue-eyed grass and, near the earth but still visible through the tall grass, reddish leaves of wild strawberries. The saturation colors of flowers and grass are due to the climate, which is seldom extreme, with a warm but not hot sun in summer and a winter tempered by the surrounding water. The fog that often drifts over the island protects Grand Manan from the droughts that trouble so much of the east coast of North America, and the vegetation is luxuriant.

We sat in the middle of the fortunate field, soaking up the colors and the mixed fragrance, and eating tart-sweet straw-berries. At the edge of the field was a weathered house ran-domly spreading into ells, storerooms and barns. It appeared as old as the fields and rocks. Tranquillity was never-ending here. High in the sky tree swallows, steel blue on the back, pure white below, appeared to be blown by the wind, adding to the sense of carefree ease. The swallows were not as pur-poseless as they looked. This species breeds in wooded swamps, nesting in hollow trees, and for their insect food they need open space. The windblown-leaves effect is in reality a swift darting, banking and swooping. Probably there were already young in the nests, as the tree swallow is an early nester. The effortless-seeming birds, so quick that the eye could not follow their course, had to spend every waking minute working for their progeny. This fine-weather day they fed high, where the food was. In bad weather, when the insects descend, they skim low over ponds and often surpris-ingly far out on the bay. The tree swallows work hard, and on Grand Manan they were by far the most numerous of the four kinds of breeding swallows. (Seeing them in migration one autumn day near New York City, I realized the immensity of their numbers: up to one hundred thousand migrate at a time. Clouds of them darkened the sky. Every bayberry bush was covered — they will eat bayberries and other kinds of berries when the insect population dies off.)

Two pairs of bobolinks flew over us, the males singing

their long beautiful warble with intensity. It was good to see them, because in our home area they have declined almost to nothing. They need open meadows like this one for their ground nests, and avoid the New York City region. Many fields have become housing developments, and the few that are left are hayfields. Early mowing killed most of the birds and their young. The nests, in untouched fields like this, are almost impossible to detect. The brooding female walks some twenty feet from her nest when disturbed, and returns the same way.

Though both tree swallow and bobolink need plenty of space, tree swallows have accepted the companionship of man, to the limited extent that they will nest in a box put up on a pole in a backyard. The bobolink, unable to nest in confinement, goes where there are no backyards and there meets mowing machines. Sometime, probably fairly soon, it will not have anywhere to go along the Atlantic coast.

We had eaten enough strawberries and walked down to the beach, an arc of gray sand enclosed by boulders. It was near low tide and rock ledges were exposed far out, covered with harbor seals, dry and yellow from sleeping in the sunlight. We counted fifty on one ledge; there were probably many more out of sight. We picked our way out toward them but they didn't wake up and we didn't get very far. The boulders were coated with slippery rockweed, the tough brown algae of the shore that can withstand alternate surf and sun. Grand Manan's particular rockweed is bladder wrack, which ordinarily lives on surf coasts. It is short and thick, and has great tensile strength to withstand the pounding of waves. Here the tide races through it, though there are few real waves, and it clings to rocks with its own self, as if a part of it had turned into cement. At the end of each frond is a pair of

45

large air pockets like leather bubbles to keep it floating. When the water recedes it is protected from the sun by its own mucilage, which absorbs and contains moisture: it is slippery on purpose.

Brown algae are descendants of some of the most ancient plants, and the rockweeds were possibly the first to colonize the shore. They rose at a time when the earth was still enveloped in heavy clouds, and as the sun only feebly and rarely touched them they could not benefit from its rays. Even now they simulate their early existence and can live only on northern coasts where fog and cloud abound. Other members of the brown algae family live deep. But draped over a rock we found a large one that had been torn from its ocean home. It was laminaria, and resembled an old oilskin. Its Greek name, *phaeophyceae,* means "dusky plants," and underwater it is dark and shadowy. It had been pulled loose by an unusually strong current and was stranded on the upper beach, slowly drying out in the sun. It looked extraordinarily abandoned. Picking it up I found it was still slimy, and there was much more to it than I had realized. It covered the large boulder and trailed indefinitely in the sand below, and by the time I had it all off the beach and organized there were about six feet of "leaf" (lamina), two or three feet broad and widely ruffled at the edges, and about twelve feet of rubbery stem. The stem was like a whip, thin at the end where it met lamina, widening to an inch or more, then narrowing to the "root," a clawlike holdfast that could have belonged to a roc. Without its lamina the stem is easy to hold and swing, but it wraps itself around one dankly. Despite the limpness, or perhaps because of it, the laminaria usually manages to survive the tide and current. Out of water it is unattractive and smelly as are most dying things, but alive in its proper element it gives with the constant flow, its holdfast gripping strongly, its spacious frond affording a home to many small sea creatures that need protection from tide and larger animals. Man benefits also, extracting iodine and other medicinal chemicals from it. Darwin remarked that the large laminaria do good service with their submarine forests to ships navigating stormy coasts. They form natural breakwaters, or act as buoys marking dangerous rocks near shore, on which they grow thickly.

Laminaria, in common with all algae, is one of the two major original divisions of plant life, the other being fungi. Stem, leaf and root are all of the same material; there is no flower or seed. The holdfast does nothing for the plant except hold it in place, and nourishment, mostly mineral salts, is absorbed from the ocean through all the seeweed's exposed areas. The most primitive algae are one-celled plants, whose ancestors were the first vegetation to appear in the earth's original shallow seas, in the Precambrian era well over 600 million years ago. These plants are the food basis for all animals that live in the water. With time, some gathered into colonies, groups of simple cells, and as with all life that exists in water, their next development was directed by water. The urge to survive in the ever-changing sea had brought them together in the first place, and the same urge dictated the slight changes in character of some cells. Water clearly ordained their shapes. To exist in a constantly moving environment the colonies had to pretend something like roots to cling with, to keep them from drifting to dry land or deep sea, where they would die; something like leaves to let the water stream around and through without tearing them apart; something like a stem to hold leaf and holdfast together and give with the current. A contradiction developed: one-celled plants, clinging to one another, barely differentiated, achieved elaborate structures attuned to the inconstant environment of waves, sand, sun, rock. The well-arranged colonies weave easily, clinging to rocks if need be, withstanding the buffeting of most storms. They are surrounded entirely by an element that contains every nutrient they need for food. They suffer neither from drought nor rain, and they do not need undiluted sunlight. Though a few are washed up on beaches, the ocean floor and the intertidal zones are dense with live plants, home and food for many sea animals. These ancient organisms are remarkably durable, adapted to and shaped by their native element as few land plants can be. The laminaria in my hands, untimely dead, gave evidence of the toughest life.

In contrast to the simple and enduring life of the tide zone is the bog back of the beach, beyond the flowered field, an area so specialized that it is, in its short life span, entirely self-contained. Once you set a foot on it you forget sea, field and forest. There was once, in this place, a lake. On its shallow borders rushes grew and died, decomposing into peat for the support of sedges. These grasslike plants took root farther out, underwater, and died in their turn. Finally the lake was totally invaded, and sphagnum moss, which grew readily on the dead grasses, made a thick carpet. Alive, sphagnum is lacy and pale green. Dead, it is a light brown, springy mat capable of retaining a large amount of water, so that no matter how thick the mat, it is always wet, the water absorbed from the lake that still exists below. The bog is a floating mass, not quite land, only part water, the embodiment of life in decay contained within the old lake shores. When one jumps on it, a person a few yards away can feel the "earth" move in heavy ripples. In a few places along the edges, where sphagnum has not yet taken over, there is new grass, thick and very green, and before you know it your feet are sucked under. We never went alone into the bog.

In other spots we could see the beginning of the end: the herbaceous cover, mostly plants of the heath and huckleberry families, supported by sphagnum, had itself rotted and formed true soil, rich and firm enough for trees. Spruce and larch, still young, were growing in groups of four or five, taking for nourishment the water not far beneath. Soon there would be bigger trees and less water, and then there would be a forest on dry land. We visited other areas designated on the maps as bog and found heavy new woodland with only here and there a trickle of the old bog, a line of sundew or a single orchid.

This bog near the shore was evidently at its prime and had a lush appearance entirely at variance with the latitude. Crowberry formed a carpet above the sphagnum, and swamp laurel and Labrador tea abounded. Swamp laurel, closely related to mountain laurel, is smaller, and its clusters of elegant flowers are veined with dark pink on the inside. Labrador tea has fragrant white flowers, much smaller than laurel, crowded between narrow rusty leaves. Rhodora, or wild azalea, and swamp huckleberry were in bloom; the rhodora deep magenta, the huckleberry pink-white and demure, heads down like little bells. Beside and among the heath and huckleberries there was a multitude of smaller flowers supported by the thick sphagnum cover. Scattered in profusion were the shining white wide-open blossoms of baked appleberry, also called cloudberry, a member of the rose family. Where the five petals had dropped off five sepals remained, saturated pink. Sometimes they were closed around the berry, which later in the summer becomes amber-colored, a few grains, like a small raspberry, tasting, it has been remarked, "more like a half-decayed than a well-baked apple."

One of the commonest bog plants raised hundreds of white downy heads over the creeping vegetation. That was swamp cotton, neither a flower nor a grass but a showy sedge. It was at its most ornamental now in early summer, having shed its small spikelet of flowers and gone to seed, its cloudlike "fruit" high, waving with an occasional breeze. In the Arctic, Eskimo women pluck the soft heads and spin them with their fingers into wicks for their seal oil cooking lamps.

Wild lily of the valley grew in the shade of shrubs, much like its domestic relative but with minuscule flowers forming into a spike on the erect stem. Along the edges of the bog, beyond the original lakeshore, grew blue flag: a wild version of the iris, Greek for rainbow, so named because of its wide color range. Those on Grand Manan were violet to pale blue, but other members of the family have an almost infinite variety of hue. A white iris was chosen, it is said, in the twelfth century, by Louis VII of France, as his royal emblem, and *fleur-de-lis* is believed to be a contraction of *fleur de Louis*. On Grand Manan the blue flag came out all at once, all over the island, in wet or dry places, sun or part shade, at the same time as the wild strawberries.

Just starting to bloom was grass pink, also known by its genus name *Calopogon,* which means "beautiful beard" in Greek, and refers to the golden bearded lip of this northern orchid. It seemed rare to us, as it occurred only infrequently, all by itself, a sparkling pink orchid, two or three one-inch blooms on one stem, a single leaf like a blade of grass, the whole miniature creation seeming to have been transplanted to a cold country from a jungle. The high season of plentiful calopogon was said to be later, from the end of July to the middle of August, and then some islanders and summer people used to go into the bog and pick it in large bunches.

We have been there many times, all through the summer, and calopogon no longer has a high season. It is here and there, single plants, hard to find. After a while the little orchid will vanish entirely, like some of the lovely, plentiful flowers of childhood — trailing arbutus, trillium, lady's slipper, fringed gentian — which one now rarely sees in their native woods and fields. I found one calopogon pulled up by its roots and left to die on the pale sphagnum. It was still bright and I took it up as if it were a wounded pet, reflecting on the pointless destruction which is attractive only to the human race. Its stem was broken so I could not replant it, but I got it home, revived it in water, and pressed it between the pages of a book which I planned to read but did not, because of the frail enclosure. Perhaps some day this will be the single specimen of calopogon from Grand Manan. It is a terrible thought.

One of the bog's more complex inhabitants is the carnivorous pitcher plant. Exotic as it looks, it does not seem in danger of extinction yet. Few would be likely to pick it in bunches; yet we saw, in a vase on a piano, an entire colony that someone had hunted up and picked. It resembled, as expected, dried-out red and green toadstools. It is difficult to fathom the motivation.

Other safety factors of the pitcher plant are its choice of extremely wet patches of bog where no one would walk for pleasure, and its habit even there of hiding under larger, denser plants.

We first found only the leaves, almost invisible under the creeping crowberry. The flowers were not yet out. The leaf is a fat little reservoir, narrowing toward the top to resemble its name. The pointed top is curved inward and has honey glands which are the first step in the damnation of a hungry insect. Among the honey glands, on the inside of the lid, are hairs pointing downward. The feeding insect, having got in, cannot get out again, but is doomed to eat until it dies. Feeding downhill, it reaches the rim of the reservoir. There the hairs stop at a glossy surface which affords no footing. Down slides the insect, landing in a pool. It drowns, gradually dissolves and becomes part of the nitrogenous food on which the plant depends. On a small scale the insect's fate brings to mind a Hogarth series. However, the story has another side. The drowned insects also furnish food for the larvae of a fly which later on enters the blossom (not the deadly leaf) and assures cross pollination.

The pitcher plant's flower, which we saw on another visit to the bog, does not look so much grotesque as artificial. The sepals and petals — green, purple and deep red — curve inward, overlapping in heavy folds like a double umbrella, to protect the yellow style. The folding petals and the flower's drooping position protect the pollen from rain and wind, but carrion flies, among its pollinators, are attracted by the dead meat colors and find entrance easy. Once blooming had started we found dozens of these obese yet handsome plants, in colonies, each with its cluster of stout pitchers, which had been green and were now veined with bright red, surrounding the single straight-stemmed flower. They looked like flamboyant arrangements in wax.

Another carnivorous plant in the bog was sundew, attractive and deadly. Its thin red stems spread spiderlike, flat on the ground, a small round leaf at the end of each. (The red is so intense that the sap will stain paper.) The leaves have a dewy look, and in fact they exude a gluelike liquid. Around the circumference of each leaf are many fine, strong hairs. When an insect alights to feed — a small insect, as the leaves are not more than three quarters of an inch in diameter — these tentacles close in from all sides and hold it fast. The fluid which was so enticing now becomes acid and contains a digestive aid which destroys the tissues of the victim. Gradually the food is absorbed and the hairs open out again, exposing the flat moist little leaf innocently to the sun. Everywhere we looked sundew spread at our feet; we could not avoid stepping on it. Blackflies and mosquitoes are a menace all over the island, but the bog, wet, hot and windless, seeming a natural habitat for every kind of insect, was free of them. There were not even swallows in the air. Hundreds of thousands of sundew leaves took care of that. If an insect strayed in by mistake it could not even attack a sundew. Its glands serve for defense as well as nourishment. There is a kind of moth that can live on the leaves, but nothing else can. What insect would want to live on a sundew anyway?

Everything about the sphagnum bog was clean except the unfinished edges, which were as dangerous as muskeg. The multitudinous flowers were immaculate, untouched by any sort of blight. The only animals in evidence were white-tailed deer, which fed on the laurel (supposedly poisonous to sheep). There was little birdlife. We found one bird's egg, probably that of a swamp sparrow, one of the few birds that prefers to nest on wet ground.

The bog was a world of purity. We wished a high fence could be put around it.

4.

We walked a track behind another of the rare sand beaches on a day so foggy that the dunes took shape only when we pushed through sharp-edged dune grass, wet to our waists, to climb them and see the calm mist-covered bay beyond. Dimly we saw a few sandpipers and semipalmated plovers, the small black-collared species that nests from the Arctic to here, its southern limit.

Even though the dangerous herring gull population was small along this beach there were not many birds. Most of the small shorebirds breed from the subarctic up through the coldest Arctic, after a tremendous migration from their homes in South America. On their way down, later in summer, they hit Grand Manan, an island in a waste of sea where they can rest and eat for a while.

Going back to the sand track we found that it followed a lake, Long Pond, which, at the flood tide, would be inundated with sea water. A few dowitchers (heavyset sandpipers) fed at the reedy edge, their long beaks jabbing the mud with mechanical rapidity. They must have been still in migration, as they nest only in the interior of the Arctic, along the shores of Hudson Bay. We could see nothing beyond them. The world was an imagined place, like an artist's sketch, with a few strokes that indicated a rowboat, charcoal smudge of a clump of pines, penciled lines of dune grass not ending sharply but fading into whiteness. Foghorns sounded unevenly from everywhere — coast and islands — muted by distance. There was no other sound. Two flashes of color shone through rolling gray fog. Towering over the dune grass was an ornamental, oversized plant called false arnica. The flowers resembled enormous bright yellow asters, the leaves could have been overgrown romaine lettuce made of leather, and the stem was almost an inch through. Thickly as it grew there — tall healthy clumps with hundreds of sunny blossoms — it exists nowhere else in New Brunswick and was not even formally discovered until 1881. It made a fine show in the surrounding dimness.

In Long Pond, behind the beach, grew spatterdock, or yellow pond lily. It is a member of the water lily family, but it is not much considered. In England it is known as brandybottle for its shape, or frog lily because it lives in the mud of shallow water. Though botanists look down on it, it is a good bright yellow on the edges of the pond, where nothing else grows but reeds.

A third flower we smelled before we could see it — the rugosa rose — and all the beach was permeated by its fragrance. Its bushes grew as high as six feet and were profuse with heavy deep pink blossoms among thick shining leaves and thorny branches. Though an Asian import it has escaped from gardens and spread widely along the northern beaches, thriving on salty wind.

On the track between beach and pond appeared clearly visible evidence of the reason for the silence and absence of birds: at first there were single tracks; then, as we followed them through the dunes and onto the beach, several, probably those of a family. They were the confident tracks of gray foxes, walking, not running. The area is the only wildlife refuge on the island, and one of the few remaining fox families had found it and taken sanctuary. Everywhere else we walked there were empty cartridge cases, but none here. The foxes were safe as long as their food supply lasted, which would not be long. Gulls did not nest here; only a few rested silently on the lakes, taking time off from the endless fight for food. The only permanent inhabitants appeared to be eiders. Off in the foggy sea were possibly a hundred males, conspicuous in their whiteness. A few drab-feathered families of females and young paddled near shore, well away from the handsome males. Other beaches had hundreds of young eiders and thousands of herring gulls, but Long Pond was no sanctuary for birds. As soon as all had departed the foxes would be forced out too, to face the inevitable buckshot from the island's relentless hunters.

As we walked back the capricious fog lifted for a few minutes and the far side of Long Pond was visible. On a tall dead tree perched a bald eagle, his white head shining against the dull sky. He watched us constantly until the mist came down again, but he did not move. He was safe here; nothing would attack him, and his favorite food, small fish, was right below him. It is remarkable that a bird so obviously predatory, with vicious talons and a heavy down-turned beak made for slashing, should be so mild and even cowardly in its habits. Ospreys and some small hawks can easily turn the bald eagle out of its nest or chase it in the air and force it to drop its fish; and as for hunting the eagle would rather pick dead fish off the beach then dive for live ones. The Long Pond eagle, who lived there always, with his family, led a life as nearly perfect as his breed could find. Like the foxes, he had found his refuge.

Much of the east coast is as untouched as Long Pond. There is only one ugly beach, Castalia, which has a picnic ground and trailer park in the middle of it, an unsanitary yellowish area roped off for swimming on its accompanying bay and marsh, and a hideous line of rusted old cars at the far end. People drive along the dusty or muddy little road, never pausing, just out to drive. Trucks dump earth and rocks from new foundations, and it is impossible to walk without getting dirty from the spray of the motor vehicles and being preyed on by the swarming millions of insects which live there from June until September, whatever the weather.

However, we walked it frequently, sometimes twice a day. Its fascinations were unending. The first attractions were the bank swallows that nested in the sand banks at the near end of the beach in great numbers. They were a busy lot, quick as bats and not much bigger, diving into the hordes of insects, swooping out again and back into their nest holes, remaining there a scant two or three seconds, then off again to the beach, buzzing all the time. The bank swallows' burrows, some at eye level, most higher, were deep, slanting down two to three feet in the steep cliff, and lined with grasses and feathers. Once in a while a bird rested on the smoothed edge and the dark breast band was easily seen. When they flew they were so fast that one noticed nothing but the drab brown of the back and wings and the off-white of the belly. The bank swallow is not the most beautiful or musical of birds but its activity is wonderful and its deeply excavated, careful nests are neat little marvels of architecture.

On the well-traveled beach road we encountered, one day in July, a single spotted sandpiper, rocking easily, quite at home. We were within two yards when it flew low along the ground on stiff wing beats, calling with two urgent repeated notes. A spotted sandpiper is a usual bird on Grand Manan, but it was unusual to find one in the same place on the same road for several days running. After a while it took to coming out of the dusty grass by the roadside, much more alarmed than it had been. It flew only a short distance, then descended and walked, dragging its wings and crying, apparently panic-stricken. It is a good tactic, probably unconscious, but we knew it, and found the nest: shallow, lightly built of grasses in the center of a young thorny rugosa rose bush. The eggs were pale, mottled unevenly with chocolate, and they blended with the shadows of the grasses and the bush. Even when we looked right down at them, parting the heavy cover, it took a few seconds to know they were there. We did not see them hatch. One has to be standing over the nest at the very moment. The birds break out of the eggs fully feathered, walk right out of the nest and pick up their own food. They scatter widely, returning only at night and in cold weather, when their parents protect them. The sandpiper had chosen its place wisely, without fear of the continuous human traffic or the depredations of gulls. We were the only ones who knew it

58

Brush weirs offshore look as natural as if they had grown there. Most are only reminders of the past, but a few are still used.

was there, because we were on foot. No gulls could discover the dense hiding place of the nest, and the hatchlings are invisible in the thick grass. Squirrels, populous in the woods, cannot live on the treeless beach. There was the danger of rats, but there is that everywhere.

Evening at Castalia is the best time, while it is still light and the birds are coming in from wherever they have been in the daytime, to eat and sleep. In late July, not long after the spotted sandpiper's nesting had finished — we hoped successfully — we walked down the road in a light fog. Before, there had been several nights of bright moonlight, around the full of the moon, the time that migrating birds prefer to travel. This misty evening was entirely devoid of drivers, and given over to birds. Down on the beach were clouds of small sandpipers and plovers, more than we have ever seen anywhere, possibly in the hundreds of thousands. There were the sound of wings and the continual sweet calls as dark flocks swept along the beach, circled, rested, circled again, not yet ready to settle. This was part of the great horde out of the Arctic, on its way to South America, pausing one foggy night on the only land for miles. They flooded over the beach like a tidal wave, crossed barely above our heads to the marsh and swung back again in never-ceasing sound and motion — a beautiful invasion.

Clear through their little calls came the long twisting song of a purple finch. He sat on the top of a dead spruce, in the one thin clump of wasting trees, at the picnic ground by the murky swimming place. He was drab, like a streaked sparrow, and did not look quite finished, but his whole body pulsated with his perfect song. It was not the time of year for bird songs. This young one, not even grown his red neck and head feathers yet, apparently sang simply for the joy of finding out that he could.

In the shallow bay three great blue herons, fishing in the mist, seemed even larger than they were. All three stood in a line, still as images, on one foot, the other bent slightly behind, head and beak pointed at the water. Around them other shore-birds had finished eating and were asleep: dowitchers, yellow-legs, black-bellied plovers, their heads tucked into their wings. They too were migrants, and the bright breeding plumage was streaked, turning into the gray and white of winter.

One among them was not ordinary: a stilt sandpiper, long-legged and delicate. In fact it should not have been there at all, as it migrates through the Midwest hundreds of miles away. It was not yet asleep — possibly nervous at being in the wrong place? — but walked around in the shallow bay, some-times up to its breast, probing the mud with its slender beak, back and forth, or kicking at the water with pale green legs to stir up the insect larvae and small mollusks that it loves. It stood out from the fat dowitchers and tall yellowlegs like a twenty-year-old at her aunt's bridge party.

5.

*C*astalia is the only beach used constantly by Grand Manan's human population. Most of the east side of the island is lonely, though it is there that everyone lives. Agriculture is on a minor scale, consisting of a few kitchen gardens. Dairy farming, once widely practiced, has vanished almost to nothing. The number of cows has decreased to the extent that the one milk processing station has ended its activity. The grass of the pastures, always green from fog and dew, has grown tall, and trees are beginning to take over, along with large patches of raspberry and blackberry. Between the five small towns there is only an occasional house. Nearly the entire male population is out at sea a major portion of the year, pursuing the island's one lucrative industry. Before the big fishing fleet was built, which happened only after seawalls were constructed way out in the harbors so anchorage was safe, the fishermen depended on handline fishing from rowboats or slightly larger skiffs, and on brush weirs.

There are probably a hundred of these graceful structures along the coast, many merely reminders of a past day: broken lines of saplings with seaweed caught on them, perpendicular to the shore and ending in a large trap curled inward on itself so the fish can get in but cannot easily find the way out. Only a few are still used, owned cooperatively, named and regarded with the affection others have for a boat. They have a natural look to them, as if they were extensions of the shore. The saplings, mostly tall young birches, are new and continuous, and their close-growing branches have been left on, and wave in the wind as if the trees were really growing there. At low tide it can be seen that they are bound to stout spruce logs. Then, too, the fine net is visible, seaweed in its meshes. The trap is an unbroken sweep about two hundred feet out, its incurving ends not quite touching the straight line of net-strung trees that connect it with the shore.

Unprofessional as they appear, brush weirs are one of the oldest methods of catching small herrings and probably the most ingenious. Whoever thought of it must have thought himself into the mind of a shore-browsing young herring. Adult herrings come near shore at the time of spawning and lay their eggs, about thirty thousand per fish, in a place where the young will grow safely, unthreatened by the predators of the herrings' normal deep waters. The little fish feed along the shore, placidly swimming around obstacles. The weir seems just another natural obstacle. They turn out to sea along the brushy line of trees and, instead of finding themselves on the other side, end up inside the trap. Even then it is not evidently a trap; it is large and similar to the shallow coast to which they are accustomed. The weir owners go out in rowboats near low tide, to cross and recross the trap trailing a lead weight. If enough fish bump into it (and, astonishingly, they do) the narrow opening is closed off with net. Now, if the young herring has an identifiable thought, it must know it is caught. Wherever it turns it finds another herring, and there is a constant swirling of crowded bodies.

A fine sunny afternoon, one of Grand Manan's rare days, we went out aboard a carrier that belonged to a weir partner, for the catch. The ocean was at half tide, and ahead of us was a pumping boat towing a skiff. A pumping boat is actually a lobster boat with a superstructure laid on it for the weir fishing. The lobster season ends in early July, but the handy boats have other uses. Weir fishing can take place only in summer, so any lobsterman with a boat can rent it to anyone else with the pumping equipment, in a sort of Cox and Box arrangement where nothing overlaps. The curving line of saplings was nearly out of water when we arrived, and the top of the net was exposed. In the skiff was another net, a black purse net, fine-meshed, with orange floats to keep it up. It looked small and flimsy, folded in the rear of the boat. Two men slowly circled the inside of the weir in the dory, letting the net out and fastening it at intervals to the stakes. The slack was fastened to the pumping boat. Now it seemed immense, a black web circling the little fish. The carrier we were on followed the two boats into the weir and was roped touching the side of the pumping boat.

The weighted purse had fallen to the floor of the bay, as it can do only near low tide. Now it was pulled close at the bottom with twine woven into the mesh, to prevent the fish from slipping out under it. Two more men joined the two in the skiff and these four drew the net in, slowly, pulling in unison, their faces tautened by the effort, lips drawn back. Below them were flowing rivers of fish, not yet panicked, weaving back and forth in the darkness, crossing lines, sometimes surfacing in flashes of silver.

The immediate excitement of hard work takes over. As the net closes, the skiff moving closer to the pumping boat, the fish begin leaping high into the air. Some of them are caught by the gills and flail helplessly in the mesh until one of the net pullers throws them back in. They are a quivering, solid mass. The men heave a large black rubber hose about one foot in diameter over the side of the pumping boat and the pump sucks bright fish into it, up to the top of a wooden chute. There is a rough wire screen that, as the fish whirl over it, removes their scales. They stream — no longer bright — down the chute into the carrier's holds.

With them is one horned sculpin, spined from its overlarge head to its skimpy tail, one skate that looks like a huge underwater bat, and a lot of fine mackerel. There is no procedure for dealing with mackerel on Grand Manan, as the catch is relatively small, and these beautiful fish will go to the fertilizer plant except for the few the crewmen lay aside for dinner. The skate and the sculpin are left to die, though they could have been thrown back. These fish, however unattractive, are useful scavengers. Though they eat small fish and crustaceans they also scour the ocean floor for dead marine creatures, which they devour entirely, their digestive regions being tough enough not to be hurt by spiny backbones. Most fish, attempting to eat their own dead, would be killed by the sharp contact. A shark is a different matter, a primitive danger to all marine animal life, and if there had been one it

As the purse net is slowly drawn up by the weir fishermen, herrings leap out and the rivers of fish become a silver flood.

would have been fished out with a large hand net and killed. If there had been a seal it would have been chased out of the weir, or shot. Seals are protected unless they are caught in a weir. It would seem irresistible for a seal to live in a weir, and the reason not more are found there is that they are fairly intelligent and probably recognize weirs as human territories.

As the fish pour into the holds a man throws salt on them by hand, approximately one 80-pound bag per hogshead. A hogshead is itself an approximate measure, in this case about seventeen hundred pounds. The carrier has two holds, with twenty-six hogsheads in each, and they were filled entirely within an hour. When full they were covered with the last of the salt, like snow fallen on the dead, scaleless bodies.

In the meantime, on the pumping boat, its two managers, the older seventy-nine, the other not much less, take care of the scales. The scales come down a zigzag chute from the top and pour out through two exits on deck, which can be opened and closed by hand, alternately. The never-ceasing flow goes into coarse wicker baskets weighing sixty pounds when full. The two old men carry them, set them down, heave them up again when the scales have settled, and empty them into other partly full baskets. They talk little but seem cheerful. "Maybe I'll make enough today to get to Expo," says one. A little later, while lifting a full basket on top of two others, he remarks, "I'm not supposed to lift things." The other turns, with a question. "Doctor says," answers the first man matter-of-factly. They are both very thin, and the muscles on their necks are like cords. They are in the pumping business only for the scales, for which they get thirty to forty thousand dollars a year, at eleven cents a pound. Fish, live or dead, never touch the pumping boat, being transported from water to carrier hold in covered conduits. But scales are everywhere, in our hair, on our hands, clothing, shoes. They make a lovely sparkle but stick like glue. They are used in the manufacture of artificial pearls and luminescent paint. In the baskets, as they settle, they cling to each other in shining sheets.

One of the old men takes time off to explain that things are easier nowadays. There used to be no sucking tube; instead the fishermen bailed the herring from the net with baskets into their dories, where they were emptied on the floor of the boat. Descaling was done by wading among them, the scales falling through the floor boards, to be collected later. These men are old enough to regard the present process as mechanized. To us it appears to demand intense physical labor on the part of every one of the nine or ten men. And all are past middle-age except one twenty-year-old. The faces of the net pullers, both in the dory and the pumping boat, have a similar expression. They might all be related. Even the youngster is part of the breed. When in momentary repose, their mouths turn down at the corners and their eyes are narrow. But they are not grim; they are intent, watchful, serious. They see and pluck out every fish that catches its gills, they look constantly for holes, keep the net steady and even, or divided if necessary. The few words they speak are question and instruction.

When the holds were full the net handlers loosened one side to let out what seemed an unending river of fish. They looked like laminaria streaming in the current. But there were still too many left; just under water light seemed to play on silk. The carrier departed, heavy, to the mainland. But we couldn't go. The purse net was still full of fish, and many were floating, dead from being confined in so small a space. They had not enough oxygen, and perhaps many died of shock.

Herring gulls were very much with us, aggressive and greedy. They kept picking up fish and dropping them. Once in a while one would manage to swallow its fish in one gulp.

More often the gull that had dropped the fish would swoop down on it, followed by three or four others. They would all pull angrily at the one small fish, wings flapping, while around them free fish floated. Between arguments the gulls sat on the weir posts, those few that had flattened tops. Sometimes a gull couldn't quite make the perch, scrambling at it with webbed feet, finally landing on its stomach. Those that couldn't get privileged positions, either on the posts or the decks of the boats, landed on the weir net, where they looked like uneasy tightrope walkers. A young one fell between two nets and it seemed certain that he would break his wings in the effort to flap up again, and die there. Finally, by mistake, he came to the place where one net ceased, and instantly he was in the water. As we watched he tried to rise, and finally made it, winging unsteadily away, faraway. He was very young, probably hatched this summer.

Before leaving the weir the carrier's owner had radioed North Head for another carrier. He couldn't leave all those fish there. The dead ones, quickly increasing in number, would sink to the bottom and contaminate the weir indefinitely. There were not enough sculpin to deal with them. Though it was the best catch of the summer he was worried. Weir owners cannot make as much as the seining boats, which go wherever they want, where sonar tells them the swarms of fish are greatest, and drop their own purse nets, which are then pulled in by winch. We had seen the crew of one of these seiners, a great boat of one hundred and ten tons, with a hold capacity for two hundred hogsheads (they had never attempted that much; on their last catch, of far less, the boat was awash "a foot," said one of the crew). That was a crew of small thin young men who had never been exposed to the strenuous handwork that went into weir fishing. All they needed was not to be seasick. They pushed buttons and had food cooked on a stainless steel stove much more elegant than any we had seen on the island, and kept hot in deep, covered warming ovens. If one of that crew makes only $250 for a five day trip he thinks he has been cheated. The weirs, on the other hand, are fixed in place, and it is largely a matter of luck if herring enter one or another, or none at all. In addition the nets have to be taken up in fall for cleaning and mending; then they are stored because the fierce winter winds would rip them. In the wintertime these elderly men all go out handline fishing, which is not the fishing we think of as sport. They generally leave about five in the morning and get back near ten at night, no matter what the weather. The lines are heavy, weighted with large stones and equipped with hooks the size of a finger. They get pollock, cod, haddock and other bottom-feeding fish, and they have to know what is what, for the pull of the current and the weight of the stone feel like a fish on the line to the novice.

Left in the weir waiting for another carrier, we looked around us. In the excitement of the catch we hadn't noticed the changing scenery. The small green island near the weir had become a tall island with mud on its flanks; and North Head, which had been clearly visible when we arrived, had disappeared behind it. The tide was at dead low. Woodwards Cove, to the west of us, was a basin of mud, and old smoke-houses sagging in the middle stood high on stakes, leaning with age and neglect. The weir poles towered above us, immensely bigger than they had looked from land. The whole weir area seemed to have expanded; we were in a tall forest of spruce stakes and branched saplings, with the nets like lianas drooping between them. The sun was low beneath a dark cloud, and on the opposite horizon, just beyond the green island, a rainbow touched. One could have walked to the place where it met land. Myth seemed real here, with gulls brushing our heads, and the serious fishermen examining the net while they rolled cigarettes, and the two old men endlessly pouring their molten streams of quicksilver from one handmade basket to another, and the shining fish disappearing and reappearing in the water. Two herrings which had escaped in the deliberate loosening of the net had mistakenly found their way into a floating cardboard container, which wavered all over the weir, a pair of tail fins propelling it like a little motor. They couldn't escape, and hours later we still saw it flopping off into the sunset with a gull following closely, dipping every now and then to pluck at the tails. The full carrier, on its way to the mainland, was so low in the water it looked in the distance to be nothing but a mast floating on an empty sea. A good thing the weather was fair. In the weir the two old men varied their basket-emptying by raking the surface of the water with a primitive three-pronged fork to remove the floating rockweed that always drifted back in. Nothing was of the modern world.

Two more carriers came and went away loaded to the gunwales before the last fish was taken out of the purse net. There were still multitudes left in the weir. "We'll be back tomorrow at six o'clock," said the weir partner, "to get the rest." He had been with the weirs for thirty-five years, and his father before him. This had been an unusual take. The fish would bring fifteen dollars per hogshead, and over one hundred hogsheads were taken, fifteen hundred dollars for five hours of work. There would be more in the morning. The men looked satisfied, though so tired they were entirely silent.

The last carrier departed, several hundred herrings on its decks, residue of the overloaded holds. As it went the fish slithered down to the open spaces of the gunwales, and we saw tails at every opening, waving as if in farewell.

The pumping boat sailed slowly out of the weir and waited

beside it while the men in the skiff pulled the enormous purse net back into its neat pile, then hauled themselves around the weir again to close it, hoisting the closing nets up into the dark sky. Then they roped their small boat to the stern of the pumper and towed it to a raft, where it stayed tethered until next morning's work. The water was still light though the sky was a nighttime sky with stars. Through the cold clear dusk two lights blinked out of rhythm, Swallow Tail before us, Great Duck behind; and on the coast, house lights were on. The weir was now a mystery of foliage, and gulls floated in and out of it, still looking for forage, unable quite yet to settle down to night. The young fisherman stood on the stern silhouetted against the pale green remains of the sunset, tying up the skiff. It is unlikely that he was conscious of his effect. It was beautiful.

6.

*I*n contrast to the immediacy of the catch, the canning of the
herrings is a totally impersonal process. The fish, no longer
looking as if they had ever been alive, roll by the thousand on
a moving belt. White-uniformed women who appear as cool
as the fish swiftly cut off the heads, or more if the fish is too
long — sometimes almost nothing is left but the tail — and
pack them in cans. The remains, much more than what is
canned, drop down a chute, to be towed away to the fertilizer
factory on the mainland. The fish belt moves continuously in

a flattened circle, passing the workers at waist level and returning at floor level until all the fish have been removed. The women, paid by the number they pack, work as quickly as possible. Every fish counts. Another belt carries the cans to three intricate machines, which first let in the legal amount of oil, then cover and seal. The only sound in the factory is the loud thumping of these machines. After sealing, the cans are loaded into large pressure cookers, cooked fifty-five to sixty minutes, then washed in soda, then in fresh water, then packed into cartons. Each of the three machines processes 125 cans a minute. The number of fish in each can varies, according to their size, from four to nine. So between 90,000 and 202,500 are canned per hour in only one plant. We were given some. They were extraordinarily tasteless, and the oil left a film on our tongues. However the sale is enormous. The cartons of oily fish go everywhere, and the factories, with headquarters at Blacks Harbour on the mainland, claim to be the biggest sardine industry in the world.

A far older method of curing fish is by smoking them. The smoked herring industry on Grand Manan used to be its only way to ship out herring. It was the largest in the world in the 1850's and 1860's, and a major item in the island's economy. The fish were caught and later sent out, processed, in ships built in Grand Manan of the great hardwoods of the forest. The skill in shipbuilding has disappeared along with the hardwoods, and the shipyards have long since closed. But a few smokehouses still operate, clustered at the water's edge in the towns of Woodwards Cove and Seal Cove. The buildings are old and unmistakable, long structures with peaked roofs. Above the ridge pole of the main roof is another roof, thin and narrow. From the space between them smoke drifts slowly over the town, smelling pleasantly of fish and slow-burning wood.

Nowadays the smokehouse owner rents a boat from the mainland to catch his fish. They are conveyed from boat to plant by a rough wooden chute on which the scales are scraped off. Men gather the scales by shovel and by hand into large baskets; meanwhile the fish are dumped into large bins, where they soak in brine for three days. Then the operator, usually the owner, strings them up by the gills and hangs them in rows on wooden racks high in the smokehouse, just below the extra roof, which lets air circulate and protects them from rain. Below the racks, on dirt ground, are numbers of banked fires. These are of saltwater wood, collected in quantity on Grand Manan's accessible east coast beaches: remains of dead trees or planks from old ships, brought up relentlessly and continually by the tides. This wood, heavy from long immersion, burns slowly and flames little. The fires are covered with sawdust, to keep them even lower. It is dim in the smokehouse. Above are layers of little fish, hanging tail down, dark gold from the smoke. On the floor fires smolder, red at the cores, and the scene is a romantic view of hell.

Though smoking is a relatively relaxed method of curing fish, there are still a few things to do. Someone has to light the fires in the morning, let them go out at night, light them again the next morning, hang up new racks, examine the old. When the fish are fully cured and dry brown, after about six weeks, they are gathered from the racks and taken to the packing plant, where women, relatives of the owner, clean them expertly, squeezing the fish open with one hand, scraping the intestines out with the other. There is no waste, and the women act as if they had been born doing it. After cleaning they cut the fish lengthwise in two strips and pack them in wooden cases of ten or more pounds to be sent out to the few remaining markets. The sales have declined, as few in North America appreciate the smoky flavor of these dark little fish, and European countries have their own herring plants.

Now this industry seems slow and old-fashioned, like weir fishing, and is similarly lapsing into decay. The east coast is lined with old smokehouses, picturesquely slanting inward on themselves. Only about a dozen still operate. Even so, the report of one owner was impressive. He had nine smokehouses in Woodwards Cove. Sometimes all nine had fish; at the time we saw them five were going. One smokehouse alone can produce 600,000 fish at a time. Another owner, however, wanted to know if we knew anyone who would be interested in buying his business. All we saw were aging men, like the weir fishermen. The younger ones have found a quicker way of making money, as crew on the modern fishing fleet which brings its tremendous catches to the canning factory or the freezing plant.

It is a wonder there are any herring left, with large seiners going after them from Sunday to Friday, planes spotting schools of them, weirs trapping them, factories and smoke-houses processing them. Still the herring population is un-abating, and the depredations of man are minuscule when compared to those of sea animals. Herring is almost universally edible. Cod, striped bass, bluefish, tuna, mackerel, dog-fish, haddock, hake, finback whale (which has no teeth but baleen, a fringelike sieve hanging from its upper jaw), squid: all eat herring in all sizes from the infant a few inches long to the mature ten-inch three-year-old or the patriarch of eighteen inches. Luckily the victims are prolific spawners, some laying eggs all year round, with peaks in spring and fall. As

The twenty-five-foot drop of the tide at Woodwards Cove leaves boats grounded. From the herring smokehouse comes the aroma of fish and slow-burning saltwater wood.

mentioned, they go near shore to spawn, but they are inconstant, one year here, the next somewhere else. In one area there will be millions one time but none at all the next time the seiners go out. This was the cause, not then understood, of the occasional failure of herring around Grand Manan in the 1830's. Though the mainland government attributed it to the sloppy fishing habits of the islanders, at least one observer had an inkling that it was the herring, not man, that was unconformable. "The Herring," wrote this perceptive official, "is, in truth, a most capricious fish, seldom remaining long in one place, and there is scarcely a fishing station . . . that has not experienced, in the visits of that fish, the greatest variations, both as to time and quantity, without any accountable reason." He was not believed then, and the fact is still inexplicable. A mathematician has calculated that if a single herring and its progeny were allowed to reproduce and live unmolested for twenty years, the herring population would be 100,000 times bigger than the earth. It seems that man, however mechanized and wasteful, has not yet managed seriously to reduce this useful fish.

Herrings are necessarily cold water fish. They migrate all over the North Atlantic, feeding mainly on copepods, almost invisible marine insects with rounded bodies, jointed tails, and oar-like legs — which gave them their name — to propel themselves in a lurching manner. Copepods are the basic animal population of the sea, food for most marine animal life. They themselves live on diatoms, one-celled algae which are said to constitute 99 percent of ocean plant life. The nearly transparent diatoms, in their turn, exist most plentifully in cold water, where their necessary minerals, salts, phosphates and nitrates, are at their richest. In spring, when the light favors the growth of diatoms, they come up to be devoured by copepods, which then reproduce in uncount-able billions.

The ocean is rich, and the day will come when we will live off its plant and animal growth. We are getting there, but herrings have long ago got there. They are especially abun-dant in the western Atlantic as far south as Cape Cod, but no farther. This is the realm of the Labrador Current, a vast, slow stream that has its source in the polar basin. Cold water perpetually overflows from the Arctic Ocean, through Baffin Bay and the Davis Strait, becoming a wide river that hugs the coastline of North America, bringing with it the life-giving salts that feed the plankton that make this one of the richest fishing areas in the world. The current flows down the coast to Cape Cod; there, like the young herrings off Grand Manan, it turns out to open sea to get around the barrier. Off the tip of the Cape, in mid-ocean, it meets the warm Gulf Stream, far faster and stronger, which has swung out to sea at Cape Hatteras. The Labrador Current, being colder, ducks under the Gulf Stream and is dissipated. The plant and ani-mal life of the coast that needs cold water for survival lessens dramatically at the barrier of Cape Cod.

Off the shores of Grand Manan, washed by the polar flow, the sequence is cold water, salts, diatoms, small crustaceans, herring, cod. When we ate cod on the island we ate the north-ern Atlantic, animal, vegetable and mineral. The fishermen benefit from the same chain. Their weirs trap sardine, their seines catch adult herring, their draggers in open ocean seek the herring's inescapable companion, the cod. When the tem-perature of the water occasionally rises in summer the herring goes elsewhere and the cod follows. Grand Manan fishermen then have a thin time, as lobstering is forbidden in Canadian waters from late June until November. But they are helped by the Canadian government in the off-season, so we need not pity them.

The ecology of marine life in relation to man is so clear on the island, and so healthy, that one sees as an even greater misfortune the overfishing and chemical poisoning from industrial waste that are gradually exterminating creatures of the sea along the Atlantic coast to the south. A recent frightening development will probably affect the Canadian as well as the United States coast. Trawlers, European, Asian and American (there is a tendency to blame the Russians for this, but other fishing fleets are equally guilty) take fish indiscriminately, far offshore. Their giant nets rake in everything from the smallest cod, that should have been thrown back, to the large lobster, the twenty-five-pounder, which has survived for over sixty years. The worst immediate effect is the plight of the single fisherman with his small boat, whose whole life and support for his family are the near-shore fish that will become less plentiful in the future.

Lobstermen are better off. Canada is careful with its lobsters, with the result that the supply is still ample. Unlike the Maine coast lobstermen, who have largely decimated their lobster population by overfishing, Canadians can only set out the pots with their colorful buoys in winter and spring. This gives the crustaceans a chance to shed their shells and reproduce. Even so they have declined in the past century. Before 1850 it was much easier to catch lobsters for unexpected company than it was to dig a bucket of clams. All that was needed was a weighted hook on a line and a bit of bait, and a few hundred pounds were easily taken in shallow water. They had no commercial value because it was impossible to get them to market before they died. For a while lobsters were canned successfully, one plant at Grand Harbour receiving 625,559 pounds of live lobsters during one season.

Lobstering on Grand Manan is still profitable. The lobster fishermen bring them in to the pounds: nine vast squares, mud-bottomed, fenced in with wood slats. Each pound is about an acre in size; each holds about 100,000 pounds of lobster. They are peacefully situated along the Thoroughfare and near Ingalls Head, protected from strong wind and current by offshore islands, and the lobsters lead a lazy life, fed with leftovers from the fish factories.

We went to visit one lobster pound in August, when it was being emptied. At that time the lobsters were beginning to shed, and were nervous, inclined to attack one another. If they were not taken up quickly there would not be much left of them. A boat in the pound pulled the lobsters to the dock with a dragger, a heavy iron frame around a net. As they were passed, or thrown up on land, they literally jumped. No lethargic monsters these, though they had algae growing on their backs and didn't look in the least edible. The men examined each one with quick knowledge. A female with eggs, near her time, was put into a side enclosure to be let free later to help perpetuate her race. One with a soft new shell, limp and dead-looking, was put into another enclosure. The shell would harden in a few weeks and it would go back into the pound. Most of them were tough insects, and they were stuffed into crates, which were thrown into the water, attached by rope to one another, until the mopping up should be finished. Then they would be sent to Boston, where a great many people would find them extremely edible.

The boat with the dragging net couldn't get all the lobsters out, so the next day, at low tide, the men went out, fifteen of them, in rubber hip boots, to pick up the remaining ones by hand and put them in more crates. Low tide was at

83

dusk that day, and it was about twenty feet from the dock down to the bottom mud. The lobsters had all retreated to the last bit of water in a far corner, and their hunters looked eight feet tall in the foggy half-darkness. Voices echoed from the tall slatted walls, with sudden laughter. It was a little frightening, and I found myself feeling sorry for the lobsters.

One lobsterman, Gleason Green, successful in a smaller way, supplemented his income in the off-season by taking tourists on fishing trips or visits to nearby islands. We went with him to Kent Island, a half hour's journey from Ingalls Head. The day was warm and clear and we had the boat almost to ourselves. It was a good comfortable forty-foot boat, the *Bonney Pride,* named (but misspelled) for the small stream that is in turn named for the first white child born on the island. There have probably been Greens on Grand Manan almost as far back as Bonnys. Gleason's boat had benches all along its rear deck, and its small cabin was equipped for sleeping and eating, as are most of the island's boats. In a good fishing season no one wants to go home until the hold (in this case the ample deck space) is filled. Our captain went off course, searching for lobster pots. The season was to end the next day, and the fine for taking lobsters out of season is $250, disastrous for a small fisherman and pointless for a rich pound owner. But some of the pots are moved by strong tides from their usual positions, and Gleason wanted to help his friends by retrieving any that had strayed. He was not entirely disinterested. The usual custom is to take in the lost traps, remove and eat the lobsters and return the empty pot to its grateful owner.

Gleason didn't find any pots but we got lobster anyway. We were well out in the bay, and the wind was strong, flicking the dark blue water with white. Other boats were out too, last minute lobstermen, handline fishermen. We approached one

Cleaned lobster pots are piled near shore for the off season. In summer no lobsters can be taken from the sea, and the fine for breaking the rule is prohibitive.

boat, the twin of ours, anchored and rocking. Its captain, the apparent twin of our captain, was hauling up barrel-staved lobster pots, fat, ample traps, flat on the bottom, curved over the top. The lobsterman was, in fact, one of Gleason's brothers, and he was willing to hand over some of his catch. We got eleven lobsters. Considering the price of lobster in New York, we immediately asked how much we owed. "Nothing," said Gleason, echoed by his brother Earle. It was true. There was no catch. The lobsters were not undersized (the minimum legal size is twelve inches, at which time they are six years old and have produced their first young), and we did not later find an addition to his small fee for taking us on the boat. The Green brothers simply wanted to be kind.

Gleason played with the lobsters, setting them up on their tails so they looked like chess pieces, but before they got tired he suddenly said, "I could eat a horned sculpin," and put them in a pot of sea water. He cooked them just long enough on the little bottled-gas stove, unfolded a table in the middle of the cabin and set out melted butter and mustard pickles. We sat on the bunks around the table, six of us, and finished the eleven tender lobsters in a remarkably short time. It was a meal to remember.

7.

*A*xel and I went out to the bow of Gleason Green's boat to watch for Kent Island. The sun was warm though the sea was choppy, and we took sun and salty wind on our faces, surely one of the few absolute pleasures left. A short time later we saw a cloud of seagulls and knew that below them was Kent. The island, barely rising above the water, is a time-smoothed outcropping of rock, most of it of Precambrian origin, the substance of the earth before there was any life, one and a half to two billion years old. Over the ancient land the gulls circled and soared, playing with the wind, hardly using their wings, some so high in the air they looked like daytime stars.

More than twenty-five thousand pairs of herring gulls nest on Kent; it is the largest colony on the Atlantic coast. They were driven from Grand Manan by foxes, which were unaccountably introduced in 1874 and soon overran the island. The gulls sensibly retreated to nearby islands, openly exposed and rocky, where the foxes would not stay. There they multiplied exceedingly, usurping the space of other shore-nesting birds, notably terns. Though herring gulls have by now returned in large numbers to Grand Manan, the last time a nesting tern was seen on any of the islands of the archipelago was in 1923. The closest terns are some twenty-five miles away, on Machias Seal Island.

The reason for the survival of gulls and the diminution of other shorebird colonies (not only terns but guillemots, puffins, and razor-billed auks) is that the herring gull is supremely adaptable. It does not mind what it eats, and can live in almost all temperatures. It can even survive the depredations of humans, and in fact is one of the few species to thrive on our multiplication. It will eat anything, dead or alive, caterpillars and worms and eggs and garbage and even another gull if the victim is young enough. On Grand Manan there were swarms of gulls around the open refuse dumps, and the fish factories have, if possible, more gulls than fish.

It was low tide when we reached Kent, and Gleason rowed us in as far as he could in the dinghy. He is familiar with the island, but only as a lobsterman. Every winter he spends a few weeks there with a crew and a cook, living in the boat or, in good weather, on the edge of the island itself. They pay the cook in lobsters and they all make good money. He does not know the interior, if one can call it that. Kent is a quarter of a mile wide, covered with grass and stunted spruces. At low tide it is far wider. We were left at the edge of the tidal flat, and it was a twenty-minute stumble over seaweed and slippery round brown stones to the beach, also cobbled, its smooth stones in the slow process of being reduced to sand.

At the top of the beach was a dense small-scale forest through which we dared not pass. The island is owned by Bowdoin College, Maine, a gift from J. Sterling Rockefeller, who bought it in 1930 and set it aside as a bird sanctuary. The only human habitation is a biological field station headed by Dr. Charles E. Huntington, who has for the past fifteen years been studying the colony of Leach's petrels. We knew where the station was, but even on so small an island it was hard to reach. The woods were taboo. Their thick tangle of underbrush and moss-covered fallen trees was marked in many places with red-painted, numbered slivers of wood. These were fastened at eye level above the petrel burrows, and the earth was alive with nesting birds, unseen and silent.

Taking to the stony beach again, we disturbed the massive colony of herring gulls. They flew around us, shrieking, no longer graceful. Fledglings were all over the beach, mottled and rock-colored. Once in a while we saw one by mistake. When they stood still they were invisible in their camouflage. Though still downy and not long out of the nests, the youngsters were much more efficient than the helpless, irritable fledglings of the forest. They had to be, just as their parents had to be fierce, to forestall their cannibalistic neighbors. When we came on a chick it walked deliberately, not fast, away from us, making no sound, while a parent bird had hysterics. If water was in the way of safety it waded, sometimes even swam. When it had reached refuge it melted into the face of the rock, there, yet not there.

Above the beach, in sand or grass, we found comfortable-looking, messy nests, about a foot in diameter, of dried grass, moss and seaweed. There were two, sometimes three large dusky eggs in each nest, with dark markings all over them like a strange alphabet, blending into their background. Near a nest, in high grass, we came unexpectedly on a gull just hatched. Not much bigger than the egg it had come out of, it tottered a few steps, then crouched, motionless. Axel's heel came down not an inch from it; he had seen it move but did not know where it had stopped. I watched it flattened out against the grass roots, then carefully walked around it. The baby gull knew where its safety lay. In this case there might have been a disaster, but it could not expect human footsteps in the tall wet grass.

In all types of life there is an instinct to survive. In the higher animals this is probably as much learned as inherited. Lesson one, as the chick came out of its egg, could have been "hide yourself." We do not know in what language gulls communicate, but the parents undoubtedly tell their young how to match themselves to grass, rock and water so as to become virtually unseeable. Lesson two is probably "feed yourself," though the parents, in the first days, will feed the nestlings. They will also eat them if they come upon them away from the home territory, and what relation that has to the survival of the race is not known. Could it be a primitive form of birth control? There are certainly too many herring gulls.

We rounded a point and came on a wide inland tidal marsh. Even at low tide the marsh was ankle-deep in water. We waded through, mud sucking at our feet, and reached a field of long waving grass, scattered with white stakes. These marked more nesting sites, this time those of multitudes of Savannah sparrows, which had put together flimsy nests of dead grass deep in the live grass, where gulls could not find them. The field was crossed with straight lines of posts topped by little white houses, miniatures of the frame houses of Grand Manan, for tree swallows. They chittered at us, and the sparrows flew up, startled, before our feet. There was hardly a spot on the island where one could avoid stepping on something vital. We clung to a passage where the grass had been cropped short, and followed it to the trim buildings which house the field station staff.

It was lunchtime, and we went, stepping carefully between the nests, to wait on the west beach. We ate our sandwiches and leaned against the rocks, half-asleep in the hot sunshine and strong sea wind. Two gray seals played delightfully, like skillful children, just offshore. They arched and leaped, dove backward into the water and chased one another in undulating circles, hardly making a splash. Once in a while they rested, swimming on their backs with their black snouts in the air. They probably *were* children. The whole island was a nursery.

Near the seals' playground swam flotillas of common eiders, mothers and young in serene parade. There were no fathers there. Several hundred had moved to the other side of Kent, away from the nesting area. Brightly patterned, with glossy white backs and breasts, black tails and wings, the male eiders are far too obvious to take part in the brooding of the eggs or the raising of the young. Females and young, dull mottled brown, blend with their surroundings, be it the nest or the seaweed-filled shallow water of the coast. The adults, heavyset and gooselike, paddled between offshore ledges, the young, sometimes as many as twenty together, wheeling at the adults' examples like infantry units. An eider does not sit on twenty eggs, though she has the capacity for more than that. The number she lays is in direct correlation to what she can find to eat, usually mussels on these shores; and in less direct but just as strong relation to her predators. Her clutch is variable. Where the gull lays at the most three eggs the eider can go on and on, an example of the predator-victim chain which keeps most of the world going on in a constantly oscillating balance. "No predator," it has been written, "can afford to be too efficient."

The nest is large, of dead plants hidden under anything handy such as a low-growing spruce or a clump of grass, and generally close to a stream that runs into the sea. We found one, made of grass, liberally sprinkled with mud and lined with down. It looked so much like its mossy, muddy surroundings that only the anxiety of the mother eider duck revealed that there must be a nest there. The eggs were hatching and two dark ducklings were scrambling down to the nearest water, a trickle that would lead them to the sea. The mother duck hovered nervously over them, quacking to discourage us, until they reached open water, where they joined other broods, guarded by an adult, probably unmated or immature. The small ducks swim as soon as they are born, and very soon after they also dive. They are born with the ability to dodge and hide, and the mortality rate is low. We saw several crowds of young dive at once, preceded by an adult in charge, as a gull's shadow hit them. The dive was a little circular motion, a flip up with the head, then down, the tail following the head motion. Coming up, the hatchlings shook themselves all over, water sparkling on their down. The newest, unable yet to dive, were led by their nurse to a shaded ledge, their own color, which hid them.

Soon Dr. Huntington returned from lunch, accompanied by a biologist, Sue Billings, who was conducting a petrel-homing experiment. The staff of ten are all students, graduate and undergraduate, and each has his own project. Sue was off to inspect the woods we had not dared to trespass, and we stayed close behind, never stepping out of line.

The petrel burrows were invisible to us at first. The red markers on the trees indicated, we were assured, the nether spots where the birds hid in the dark, but all the moist green earth looked the same. Our guide, of course, knew them all, including alternate entrances. She knelt and plunged her hand underground and drew it out slowly, carrying an adult petrel.

She handed it to me, and for a few minutes I held the bird of the storms. It was dark gray and brown, about eight inches long, and soft as a mole. A small-boned, frail-appearing bird, it did not struggle but was quiet, quivering a little. The slim wings were longer than the body, and felt as if the slightest pressure would crush them.

Yet petrels thrive on all the cold oceans, north and south, no matter how rough the weather, and are the most numerous birds in the world. They come to land for a few weeks each summer to lay and hatch their one egg per pair. This is their limit, because one set of parents can raise only one nestling. They have to range far and long for food, and if there were an extra chick probably neither would survive. They hardly touch the water except for the brief dart or dive for food, and no one knows how they sleep in the winter months when they are far out on the ocean. It has been suggested that they can doze in the air, a remarkable feat. Even if it is true, they must go for a long time without real sleep.

The Kent Island species, the Leach's petrel, is so self-sufficient that it rarely follows ships, and is therefore unknown to everyone but Dr. Huntington and Sue and a few other hardy scientists who don't mind months of fieldwork in the faraway, often desolate patches of earth where these birds choose to establish colonies. Their range is limited, however, and the Bay of Fundy is as far south as they can breed. The reason is that, like the herrings, they feed on minute crustaceans which can exist only in cold water. Unlike herrings the petrels cannot migrate in the summer, being nest-bound. Even the Bay of Fundy surface warms up somewhat in sunlight, and the cold-water crustaceans go deep in the daytime to avoid the killing touch of warm water. The petrels cannot dive far down and this southernmost colony of petrels was perforce limited to night for eating. Given the proper frigid conditions petrels can feed in daylight, but around Kent they never appeared until after dark.

Naturally legends have attached themselves to birds so astonishingly at home in a hostile element. Occasionally a night watch on a ketch sailing silently has seen these swallowlike birds, dipping and swooping, chuckling at each other in the moonlight over the waves, not quite touching the water, but never more than a few inches off. They seem to be the sea come alive: dark, with a white rump patch like flung spray. When feeding or looking for food they hover, dropping their webbed feet to the surface and, seemingly, walking. So sailors of ancient times named them after Saint Peter, who walked the waves. Later European mariners, whose superstition was stronger than their religion, thought them birds of ill omen, beating up storms with their wings. Eskimos, far removed in culture, had the same concept of the petrel, but went much further, for it is a leading figure in one of their legends of creation. The petrel married a human girl and took her off to its lair of fish skins, from which she was rescued by her father. The bird, angry at her escape, raised the ocean to a fierce storm, endangering the boat in which she and her father were fleeing. The father, hardly human, it seems, tossed his daughter overboard to save himself. She clung to the edge of the boat, and the old man cut off her fingers, joint by joint. The joints became ringed seals, bearded seals and walrus. The girl herself sank to the bottom of the sea and became the arbiter, not always benevolent of man's affairs. Her father went to sleep on a beach, was washed out to sea and eventually joined his daughter. He took on the task, obviously congenial to him, of punishing female wrongdoers by whipping them and pulling out their hair. Legend does not say what became of the petrel. Perhaps it ranges over the wild oceans forever, seeking its bride.

Although the field workers knew every inch of the woods, the little birds had networks of burrows in other colonies on Kent, well concealed and largely untouched. The estimate is about fifteen thousand pairs. No one knows what enormous numbers they achieve on the northern coasts which are their favorite nesting sites.

Both mates help excavate the burrows. They use their bills as pickaxes and their webbed feet to drag and scatter the earth from the hole. To achieve this they have to lie on their sides, first one side, then the other, to make the burrow wide enough for egg, chick and often both adults at once. The pair share the incubation period, taking turns and changing over at night. It is thought that petrels are faithful for life, not only to the same mate but to the same site. One or both stay on the nest, but day or night one bird flies out to its true home, to flutter and dive in the air with its companions, seeking food and, probably, playing.

Dr. Huntington's team had taken fifteen nesting birds to places 140 to 170 miles from Kent, and they were to be released that evening. Sue was to sleep on the beach near the colony for several nights. Not to sleep, actually, but to check each of the fifteen nests every hour and note the time each lost one found its way back. Incidentally she would hear the uncanny eight-note chuckles all around her as other petrels returned from feeding, sat on the edges of their burrows and conversed with their mates. Sue's experiment with homing petrels was to last several years, and in the course of it some of the birds were sent as far away as England. They crossed open ocean, 2980 miles of it, as fast as 217 miles a day. She discovered that wherever the birds were released they found their way home over land or sea, most of it unfamiliar territory to them. How they homed unerringly without sun or landmarks is unknown. But almost all came back. Petrels are strongly attached to their nests as long as the young are helpless, or about thirteen weeks after egg laying, and have a remarkable homing instinct.

The chick is feeble and blind, and so weak it cannot hold up its head at first. It is fed continuously, night and day, the oily liquid manufactured in the stomach of the parent and regurgitated into the low-hung beak. The petrel breeding latitudes are so far north that, in the first weeks after hatching, one or the other parent has to cover the chick all the time against the cold. The egg takes six weeks to hatch, and the unfledged chick stays in the nest another seven. Toward the end, however, the parents often leave it alone, and before the nestling can fly it has been entirely abandoned. It is fat and helpless and has to exercise its wings in the burrow or, dangerously, outside at its entrance. Driven by hunger it finally flutters down to the sea at night. The Kent Island colony was close to the water, so the fledglings could make the trip to safety during one night. Birds raised more than a night from the sea have to hide in the daytime. They are pitifully easy prey for gulls, since they cannot rise off level ground unless there is a wind, and even then, still feeble-winged, they are no match for the swift and skillful predator. The gulls go over the sea to pick them off, and the young petrels, if aware in time, will dive and swim underwater, even though their wings are not adapted, like those of the auks and the puffins, for flying in the water. Alone and unguided, the young bird gradually gains strength to fly and find food. It may come on adults moulting, but ignores them and goes on to winter in waters several hundred miles beyond, still alone. It does not return to land for as long as four years, when it is ready to look for a mate.

I handed the captive petrel back to Sue, who fastened a numbered metal circlet around one thin black ankle, and placed the bird in a canvas sack. Dr. Huntington laid his jacket gently over the sack, to make sure the bird did not suffer nerves at being abroad in daylight among large strangers.

They checked another burrow. Its occupant had recently returned from an enforced journey, and Sue carefully replaced the bird deep in its burrow, on the sketchy nest of a few grasses and feathers where lay the one and a half inch egg.

The colony was closely packed, and we trod a narrow maze between burrows while the field workers checked. We left them finally at the edge of the wood and found ourselves immediately on the beach, where gulls screamed, soaring and diving, waiting for petrels. More would be hunting them at sea; indeed it was beyond imagination that such a seemingly fragile and helpless creature could not only survive but increase enormously, to populate the farthest reaches of the ocean and breed by the thousand on frigid northern or antarctic islands.

By now the tide was high, and Gleason had brought his boat close to the shore for us. In a few minutes Kent Island was a dark thin line on the water, but it lay in our minds, the tangled spruce woods and deep grass, temporary home of an elusive ocean wanderer.

Gleason took us home a different way, past a line of brown

rocks called, unaccountably, Western Green Island. Twenty-eight gray seals were sitting on the reef, watching us, curious and apparently unafraid. Gleason stopped the motor as we came close and all the seals dived off, not because of the silence but because of the change. Any change is dangerous. But curiosity got the better of them. They all swam slowly toward us, heads high in the air. If we had been hunters we could have picked them off one by one.

The gray seal is a magnificent creature, the second largest in the true seal family (Phocidae), the males reaching a length of twelve feet. They are heavy-headed, large-eyed and deliberate. They like to be together, but there are not many of them to congregate, possibly twenty-five thousand in the world. They live only near places like Grand Manan, where there are reefs and strong currents. Turbulent water is their playground; consequently they are not often come across. Once when we saw them in Fair Isle, Scotland, we were told they were very rare. On our western coast of the Atlantic they are also seldom seen and little studied. They are cold water seals, bearing their young on ice in late winter, but they do not inhabit the Arctic, as do most of the other Phocidae. Their range is restricted, from Labrador to the Gulf of St. Lawrence on the Atlantic shore, and by rights we should not have found them at all this far south. But they were there, content and curious, an almost irresistible target for a hunter. They are hunted, too, though shooting them is barred by law except, as mentioned, when they get into a weir. On Kent Island there was a constant patrol from the bird observatory to keep an eye out for boats with illegal hunters after the seals.

8.

*B*oat trips to outlying islands are few and far between for visitors, but Grand Manan itself never fails to interest, not only in its wilderness areas but in the inhabited villages. All along the east coast one is fish conscious. One hundred and fifty years ago this would not have been so. Early Grand Mananers lived in self-sufficiency. Farming, fishing and lumbering filled most of their needs. The tall forests that covered the island have disappeared long since, though there is evidence that they were there in some place names, Beech Hill

The seining fleet gets ready for the Sunday sailing. The boats will be out on the Bay of Fundy for five days, grueling even for hardened fishermen.

and Beech Tree Lane, for example. Oaks and spruces were cut for building, boats and export. When the large trees had gone the lumbermen went in for pulp logs. Now there is hardly any pulp business left. The interior of the island is crisscrossed with wood roads, but they are only vestiges, overgrown with ferns. There is still a great deal of forest, of spruce, birch and larch, but though thick and often impenetrable it is all young. Denseness keeps the trees small; they interfere with each other's growth. The second industry, farming, has died a natural death. There are still a few cows on the fertile pastures of the east coast, but orchards have grown wild and market farming has been abandoned. The climate is kind to almost any kind of vegetable growth. But the men have no time. Their business is fishing.

The fleets go out on Sunday afternoon and come back the following Friday, usually carrying a full load, up to 72,000 pounds. There are three kinds of fishing vessels, not counting the numerous rowboats and outboards. They are draggers, seiners and carriers. Draggers go far out after big fish, cod, haddock, pollock. They use coarse-meshed nylon net of vivid orange, attached to an arrangement that looks like a large iron double door. The two halves of the door are widely separated when the net is dropped overboard, then pulled together underwater to make the edges of the net meet and draw in the fish. As soon as they are caught the fish are stored in the ample holds in layers separated by cracked ice. Seiners are traveling herring weirs. Instead of waiting for the fish to come to them, they go out and find them, using sonar to detect schools. If they are looking for sardine-sized herrings they go into harbors where the young congregate. Adults, who like one another's company, are found in the bay in great schools, traveling around looking for food, or just traveling. No one knows why they move around so much except that in the summer they must move north, and that at some time they must move to nearshore spawning grounds which, as noted, vary capriciously. The seiners let down their fine-meshed black net and take in the fish in the same manner as the operators of the shore-based weirs. Carriers with two mammoth holds move all over the bay, summoned by radio from one ship to another to remove excess cargo and take it back to the fish plants.

The big boats, draggers and seiners, are expensive, usually around seventy thousand dollars, including the net, a twenty thousand dollar item. There is a net-making industry on the island, and it is a wonder to see it working. In the storeroom fine black nylon net from Japan was stacked in large bolts. Several men had drawn lengths of it into the workroom, where they sewed widths together with small even weaving stitches. Others sewed twine from British Columbia along the edges, inserting at regular intervals the lead weights and bright orange floats from Portugal. The half-finished net spilled out the door and spread all over the ground, where more men worked on it. They were making a net of ten thousand pounds, with three thousand pounds of weights and twenty-eight hundred floats, for a big new seiner. The size of the net was not to be imagined from seeing it like the accumulated webs of huge spiders inside and outside. Piled later on the dock near its new boat it was as high as a man and about twelve feet square. It matched the boat, though, looking normal when drawn up on deck by a winch. It could bring up about thirty-two tons of herring, a good deal more than the usual amount taken in the old-fashioned, graceful brush weirs.

To buy a dragger or seiner the fisherman pays one third, and the government the rest. They are seldom cooperatives. One man owns a boat and pays a percentage of the catch to the crew. After a while he pays the government back. With smaller boats, carriers and lobster boats, the fisherman can generally arrange a bank loan. The lobstermen rarely have crews, but sometimes they band together and camp out for a few weeks on one of the smaller islands.

It is easy to pass the fishing fleets on a Sunday morning without even seeing them. At low tide the seining fleet at North Head looks like a few sticks, the ends of the masts only showing above the dock. At Ingalls Head, the pier for the draggers that go out for cod and other large bottom fish, the water is barely deep enough at the docks, far out from the shore, to keep the boats afloat, and to get into one we had to descend a steep flight of stairs whose bottom half was encrusted with barnacles and green algae and looked like the ocean floor. There are other, smaller harbors all along the east coast; such as Woodwards Cove, which looks derelict at low tide, boats leaning against wharfs, their keels in mud, houses on tall stakes covered with the detritus of the sea. But these small harbors can be used by means of breakwaters far out from land. When Captain Owen sailed along the shore there were no breakwaters, and he could not see the shallow indentations as possible anchorages. The breakwaters were built by the provincial government in 1841, and thereafter larger boats could be built and fishing became almost the only full-time industry. Previously fishing had been restricted to the coast, as small boats could not survive the swells of the bay. Ingalls Head and North Head are the two best harbors, and near them are the fish factories, sardines at North Head, cod and pollock at the freezing plant at Ingalls Head.

When the tide rises the two main fleets are glorious, boats three and four deep at the pilings, masts tall, paint gleaming, orange or black net in great piles on the rear decks. On Sunday afternoon they are off, a leisurely procedure like so much on the island. Wives and children come down to the dock to gossip with each other and give their men food and moral support. One by one the boats go out to the bay, disappearing soon, not to be seen again until they come back on Friday. Five days of the week on the water can be grueling even to a toughened fisherman, and the Bay of Fundy is no lake. The heavy-laden boats can easily founder in stormy weather, and, as the water is so cold, few Grand Mananers learn to swim. One fisherman's wife remarked that, although she lived next to Swallow Tail light she never heard the foghorn unless her husband was out at sea. Then it had a terrible clarity.

Only once did we see a boat come back prematurely. We walked out to see what was the matter, and found about an acre of seining net on the dock. It had been fouled on rocks and was full of rents, some as long as twenty feet. The six men of the crew sat on boxes in the mass of net, sewing it back together again with fine stitches. One of them said glumly that it would be a good five days before they got out again, but the next day they had gone. These men are expert housekeepers.

When the fleets come in, the fish plants are particularly busy. They are open most of the week to process the fish brought in by the carriers. But the biggest loads come on Friday. We watched the preparing of a forty thousand-pound load of pollock, from ship to freezing plant. Pollock is a cool water fish, a member of the cod family, with a forked tail and a neat light stripe along its side. It is plump and greenish and grows to about three feet, weighing up to thirty pounds. Like cod and haddock it is a bottom feeder, easily accessible to the heavy nets and iron gates of the dragger. The crew of the boat, in the hold, slung the big fish into a large metal barrel which was raised to the second story of the plant by derrick. The barrel dumped them into a wooden box, they were washed, weighed, put into a vat and wheeled into tempo-

About an acre of torn seining net, fouled on rocks, lay on the pier. The crew, anxious to get out to sea again, mended it in a day.

rary storage by an agile small machine called a forklift. The unloading of this catch took forty-five minutes. Processing takes longer, though it looks spectacularly quick. The fish are filleted, skinned, cut up and packed by a rapid production line of men and women in rubber aprons to their feet, wielding ferocious knives. The fish are shipped across the street in flat cartons to the freezing plant, thence all over Canada and the United States. The fillets look like fillet of anything, flat and short and exceedingly sterile. They bear no relation to the ample gray-green denizens of Fundy.

The entrails, heads and tails and other waste are sent to the fertilizer plant, which gives off an odor extremely offensive to humans and pleasant to gulls. This plant, one of the oldest businesses on the island, used to be next to the fish factory, and it was said they could smell it in Eastport, Maine, when the wind was right, though this might be a canard put about by the residents of Eastport, who used to but no longer possess a ferry run to Grand Manan. Recently, on the complaint of local residents, the fertilizer business was moved to Blacks Harbour, on the mainland, and adds considerably to the unattractiveness of that town. In the plant men and women with apparently deadened senses of smell cook and grind the fish wastes until they produce a fine powder, one of the most potent fertilizers known and, oddly enough, almost odorless. Over all the fish works hangs a permanent cloud of gulls, soaring, floating, diving, fighting, always on the move but always in the same place.

9.

*W*e had another of the rare chances to visit a small island, and we went again with Gleason Green, to an island that can seldom be reached. The journey needs a fair day, a low wind and a high tide that comes at the right hour, not to mention an expert sailor. These circumstances came together one day in early June, and we set off for the twenty-five mile, three-hour trip to Machias Seal Island. In spite of the beauty of the day there was, as always, a swell on the bay. In a forty-foot lobster boat the smooth water looked like hills and valleys.

When we were down in a valley nothing could be seen of the horizon. Flying low up and down the hills were petrels, greater shearwaters and puffins. Petrels and puffins breed on northern islands, but the shearwaters fly all over the Atlantic in large flocks until late August, when they go to land to colonize and nest on one island in the South Atlantic. About 4 million shearwaters dig their burrows on the one square mile of the island. No man can live there, as the earth is honeycombed with burrows and gives way at every step.

There is no special drama or beauty to Machias Seal. It is no more than a jagged rock thrusting out of the sea. Even on this fair day high waves broke over the landing ramp, which we reached by rowboat. The boat washed in and out, hitting rock a number of times before we could scramble out of her. The island is very small, containing one lighthouse, a wilderness of jumbled rock and a short grassy stretch in the middle. But it attracts more than two thousand pairs of nesting Arctic terns, besides four hundred pairs of puffins and a scattering of other birds not including herring gulls. In fact this rocky mountaintop jutting out of the Bay of Fundy is all nesting area, and the visitor must confine himself to the one path through the grass so as not to tread on the eggs. Even on the path are the terns' flat grassy nests. These far travelers winter way south of the Antarctic Circle and migrate to their breeding grounds, which reach well beyond the Arctic Circle, an estimated twenty-five thousand miles a year. One can only guess at the reason for this exaggerated migration. Perhaps the birds have been pushed farther and farther in both directions over thousands of years, due to competition for feeding and nesting grounds. Or it may be a throwback to times when the climate was gentler in the polar regions, and the birds have never got around to changing their habits. Many seemingly absurd migrations are thought to be survivors of custom or necessity — habits that no longer have any meaning. But Arctic terns have more daylight during the year than anything alive. That alone could be a reason.

Wherever they land, and the Bay of Fundy is near their southern limit for breeding, the terns lay their three or four eggs per pair on bare sand or short grass, trusting to camouflage to hide the young from predators. On Machias Seal Island there were no predators, and the air was full of terns, ghostlike, slim-winged, wheeling high in the hazy sky, calling hoarsely, diving at us, circling above their nests. The lighthouse keeper said they were always like this, even when no one was walking on the island. All day and all night the keening went on. Sometimes they would be quiet for a few minutes, then one would start, and the others join in. Terns are extremely restless birds, so nervous that they often desert their nests, disturbed beyond endurance. But on this outcropping far out in the sea they managed, though complaining, to endure.

While we ate lunch, Gleason's rich fish chowder which he and two girls had cooked on the long trip, several terns kept beating at us, plucking at our hair as they brushed close. We put our handkerchiefs over our heads and ate through the angry swishing of wings and the constant harsh cries. The trouble was, we discovered later, that there were nests all around us, merest depressions in the grass, and in them were eggs varying in color, olive-gray, ashy, sometimes mottled, according to their surroundings. (In the Arctic, where they nest on sand, the eggs are sand-colored.) One nest contained two eggs, one still whole, the other broken down in the middle, where a new chick was hatching, a shapeless body of pink flesh and damp feathers. Within twenty-four hours it would be walking, fluffed out and competent. Most of the young ones we saw stayed still, well hidden by their dusty color, and moved into deeper grass only when we approached within a foot. Then they opened their beaks in soundless cries, and tried to walk on soft, unformed legs. They didn't make much headway, but we retreated immediately for fear that they might inadvertently wander too far for their parents to find and feed them.

Another summer we went again to Machias Seal and found few terns and no nests at all. There had been a thunderstorm about a week before and every chick had drowned except one, which we found hidden and shivering in the long grass, one little wing broken. On Bylot Island, where we had observed a colony of twenty nests of Arctic terns, not one egg hatched. A gang of dogs let loose by a visiting Eskimo ate them all.

Considering how vulnerable these birds are, how obvious to predators, how nervous, how long their migration, it is wonderful that they survive at all. The cause is probably the extremely wide range of their breeding territory, from Massachusetts to the northern part of Baffin Island and probably farther north, beyond the habitations of humans, all over the Arctic regions of Europe and Asia and across the whole northern part of the North American continent. Their chief enemies are gulls and jaegers, and these they avoid simply by going somewhere else. It is a joy at any time to see Arctic terns, birds of the sun.

But that day a handsome herring gull stood guard on a rock, its newly hatched young hiding under in the rock's shadow. Was this the beginning of the end for Arctic terns on the island? They had been driven off Grand Manan by gulls. Machias Seal is a sanctuary, and no living animal can be destroyed there or transported elsewhere. I wanted to secrete the chicks in my pocket and take them back to the main island, but there was a ranger nearby. He did not like the gulls either, but his stern eye was on me, and presumably they grew and flourished.

Puffins were nesting on Machias, their one chick per pair well hidden in the labyrinth of the rocks. The parents flew on short stubby wings, round and round us, their parrotlike beaks stuffed with fish, alive, tails flopping. As soon as we moved away they dived into their holes. Sometimes one stood upright for a while on a high rock, still, like a stuffed toy, white breast gleaming, black back glossy as velour, bright orange bill and feet seemingly glued on and painted.

A colony of razor-billed auks, similar to their extinct relatives, the flightless great auks, perched importantly on a shelf at the edge of the sea. Nothing worried these birds. They had laid their eggs in cliff crevices in May, and the young were already off at sea. If they could have seen into the human mind, though, they would have been distressed. They are being killed for food, feathers and fish bait, and there are not many left. The razorbill looks like a penguin, and can swim easily under water, the short wings acting as fins. Their air flight is direct, the water-adapted wings beating quickly to give an appearance of speed. Most of their lives are spent roaming the ocean, with only an occasional stop on a remote rock.

A far odder sight on the island than the pelagic birds was one cowbird and one red-winged blackbird. Creatures of civilization, one thinks, eating tamely at feeders and nesting in marshes. Here they had neither. Perhaps they had been blown out to sea and lighted on the nearest land, a desert for them. It was unlikely that they would get back home.

There are some islands one can reach without going by boat. We had heard of wild horses and cattle on Ross Island,

and went to find them. Ross is accessible on foot across one passage on the Thoroughfare (the mild inlet that contains most of the lobster pounds). It was somewhat muddy and the island itself is flat and dull, consisting of old pasture land and cutover woods. There were no cattle to be seen; undoubtedly they have long since been rounded up and eaten. The wild horses numbered three: stout, stolid ex-workhorses that looked at us mildly, neither advancing nor retreating, and continued to crop the high grass. They had got themselves a fine retiring place. On the side of Ross facing Ingalls Head is an attractive old lighthouse, now derelict, that was used to guide boats into Grand Harbour before the Ingalls Head seawall was built. Two other islands lie beyond Ross, first Cheney, then White Head, and there was a time, it was said, when one could walk or drive a wagon and horse from Ross to Cheney at low tide. But when we saw the intervening inlet, called Cheney Passage, it was low tide and the water was far too deep, even near shore, to wade or drive through. An automatic light and foghorn pursued its mechanical activities on a rock between the islands, though the weather was clear. It was a forlorn, very small machine, alone between two old mountains, with no boat in sight and no boat likely to traverse the rocky channel. It did not seem possible that it was ever useful.

Of the three islands, only one is inhabited: that is the farthest out, White Head, accessible only by the ferry that takes children to and from school. The ferry can also tow a barge with one car on it. It probably will not be lived on much longer. Its people are trickling away, depressed by the isolation of their island.

The walk back over the two or three miles of Ross was a long straight haul, only interesting when we reflected that some 350 million years ago we would have had to climb a tall mountain, and this would have been its then steep summit peak, now smoothed to a level barely above tide line.

10.

*B*ack on Grand Manan again we explored what we could of its western side. There is a sharp separation between the old, water-possessed east coast, with its lively fishing industry and its comfortable towns, and the relatively young west coast. As soon as you leave the main road, going west, you are in a different land. You climb quickly to forested heights, almost without dwellings. There are a few dirt roads and a few trails, and as you get nearer to the coast there is nothing but wilderness. The west cliffs themselves form a spectacular wall fifteen miles long and from two hundred to four hundred feet high. There are several points of access: Southwest Head by road and trail, Bradford Cove by trail, Dark Harbour by road, Indian Beach by ancient and terrible trail, and Long Eddy Light, or the Whistle, at the northern tip, at the end of Whistle Road. Whichever way you go is impressive.

We started toward Southwest Head, making a leisurely trip down the east coast. The road winds around the estuaries, coming close to the sea sometimes, at other times traversing the greenest fields we had ever seen, sometimes inhabited by vastly contented black-and-white Holsteins that seemed to be modeling for a rural painting. They lay in the green grass, and if cows could smile that is what they were doing.

When the road dipped down to the water we left the car. There were few beaches. The smooth old rock sloped unbroken into water. On it often slid the flocks of eiders so common all along that shore. Few other ducks lived on the coast, or anywhere on the island. We had seen one pair of blue-winged teal and a few mergansers. The answer is, of course, herring gulls. Eiders are the only ducks big and strong enough to fight off the gulls. In addition the female eiders leave the nests reluctantly and mostly at night, always covering the eggs before going.

Eiders have a worse enemy than gulls on the island — man. Eiderdown can be taken if one gets a license and permission from the owner of the land. This does not immediately hurt the population, as the mother bird produces three sets of the soft breast feathers which she plucks to keep her eggs warm and hidden. But between the time of taking and the time of producing more down, the eggs are uncovered and hunting gulls will snatch the eggs or, if there are any in the nest, the downy young. Three sets of breast feathers is all the eider can manage; when they are gone that is the end of that year's young. Even on an island as puritanical as Grand Manan there are pilferers, the few shiftless characters that will turn up in even the best regulated community; and eiderdown is an easy way to make money. The one ranger cannot patrol all eider areas night and day.

Though Grand Manan and the northern coast of Maine is the eiders' southern breeding limit they were numerous. We had seen them an earlier year in the northern area of their range, the land of the permanently frozen ground, treeless and chilly, but they were quite as much at home here on the gentle misty green shore. They were countless; wherever we went on the shore they swam peacefully but purposefully away, flocks of dozens, adding up all over the island, probably, to several thousand.

Also along that shore are the lobster pounds. Walking along the narrow crossways we could look to the shallow bottom and see the ocean insects creeping over the mud. There must have been some small ones in there, but all we could see looked to be five pounds or more, over a foot long.

Though they seem hardly to move, these sluggish dark green creatures rove mildly when they are free. They have a range of up to twelve miles in three days, always searching for food. This is hardly a record for a sea animal, but then, they live only on the bottom (except for the newborn, that swim at the surface for the first six days of life), and all they can manage is a clumsy crawl. If they feel they need safety beyond their own armor and strong claws, they can dig holes into which they retreat backward. Their preferred temperature is between forty-five and fifty-five degrees, and they are supremely content in the Bay of Fundy, summer and winter. There was hardly a spare inch between them as they lurked on the muddy floor of the enclosure waiting for handouts from their owners.

The road climbed through gentle fields and little towns until the land rose sharply in one of the two arms that come from the west side, enclosing the low east coast. There used to be a walk here, along the cliff, and one day we attempted it. It had been a sheep trail, and in the old days people followed it by the shreds of wool left by the sheep. But it had been many years since these animals were populous, so there were no such pleasant markers left for us to follow. We probably left bits of skin and hair instead, as the one-time trail is overgrown with dense shubbery, much of it sharp-needled or thorned. We covered our faces with our hands and often resorted to walking crouched, our knees touching the mossy ground.

Proceeding in this manner we came across a large colony of petrel burrows around the boles of trees. It was past the nesting season, and the burrows were empty. We never would have noticed them if the forest had not been so thick that perforce we kept our heads down. The petrels on Kent Island are thoroughly handled, banded, even sent off to distant destinations, but these will probably never be discovered, either by man or gull. The undergrowth was so heavy that the gulls would not find them; and the burrows, near the edge of the cliff, enabled the fledglings to flutter down at night easily and escape into the ocean. No man, having tried this trail once, would do it again, nor even find the burrows if he did, as it is long and arduous: and he would turn back, as we should have, long before. Happy petrels! Here was another reason why there are so many more of them than of any other bird — they seek out the wildest places and multiply unharmed.

Back on the road again, after taking an hour and a half to traverse perhaps a half mile, we approached the tip of Southwest Head. The quality of the land changed abruptly. It looked subarctic, with sparse, stunted spruces and the hummock formation of tundra. Shrubby cinquefoil, which also colonizes the Arctic, proliferated, covering the ground with sun-yellow small flowers. There was a lighthouse, a necessity because of the line of knife-edged reefs, hidden under high water, that stretched south far into the bay. Beyond the light was a small natural harbor, three hundred feet down a precipitous cliff with small ledges.

There we saw the few guillemots left on Grand Manan. They were in the water, some floating, some swimming under water, their orange-red legs trailing behind them, bright through the dark sea. They did not paddle, but swam with their wings, like other members of the Alcidae family — puffins, auks, dovekies and murres. From our high place the small white spot on each wing was clearly visible as they went after food (usually sand eels). Gradually they dimmed as they went down to the bottom, then slid up to the surface far away. One guillemot, a compact, velvet-black bird, was evidently trying to find a place for a nest on a downward sloping narrow ledge. It kept slipping but somehow maintained its footing. This was no mean feat for a guillemot. It is a poor walker; its legs are set too far back and its short wings, adapted to swimming, are seemingly inefficient for keeping balance. However the guillemots' preferred homes are inaccessible cliffs. They choose their nesting sites with a view to safety for their young as well as for themselves. From a cliff they can launch easily into the sea, whereas on level ground their back-slung legs and short wings make taking off virtually impossible. Awkward as they appear on land, where they go only for nesting — like petrels they live on the sea — guillemots compensate for their stubby wings with extremely good eyesight and an unerring sense of direction. They are so

Southern Cross, once part of the high western cliff, is now separated by currents which are slowly destroying the fifteen-mile-long precipice.

small and light that they do not need to be the world's most expert fliers. They can go great distances in the air on those little water-adapted wings.

The bird on the ledge twisted its head and short neck continually, like an Indian dancer. Sometimes the neck gyrated almost entirely around, the sharp-pointed beak touching the rock. It looked like an interesting exercise. There was no obvious reason, but to the guillemot it was undoubtedly vital. The motion was that of turning the eggs, but there were no eggs visible on the bald ledges. Maybe it was practicing.

Beyond the high bare ground of Southwest Head the land dipped. Now walking northwards, we entered the spruce forest which runs the length of the western cliffs. Where we walked, on a small boggy trail, the trees were short and twisted; so near the edge they were exposed constantly to wind. Just to the left of us, beyond the ragged trees, was coarse grass, then an immediate fall of sheer rock into the sea far below. A landmark stands there, near a headland. It is named Southern Cross, and in old photographs it does look like a monolithic cross. Long before photographs it was part of the cliff. The sea gently disengaged it, and now it stands well out in the water. The crosspieces have fallen, victims of wind and spray, and the natural sculpture looks like an enormous primitive woman, her arms crossed over her breast, the elbows slightly protruding. In fact her alternative name is the Old Maid. She is all the more awesome as the water around her is calm, blue, innocent. This quiet-seeming water will create more and more offshore statues, destroying them in turn, until the entire face of the cliff is reduced to its level, and the sea can inundate the land as it has done on the east shore.

A short way beyond Southern Cross a faded, hand-lettered

sign was nailed to a tree in the middle of the trail: "This is where William Jones climbed to safety. His brother Floyd was rescued Feb. 25th, 1963. Boat smashed up on beach below." The laconic notice was an eloquent reminder of the constant peril to boats off the shores of Grand Manan. The two young men had come from Lubec, Maine, about ten miles away; they ran into fog, tangled with the reefs off Southwest Head and found themselves on a narrow cobbled beach with no boat and several hundred feet of glassy cliff between them and safety. At high tide there would be no beach. The boys saw their landhold disappearing, and one of them clambered up the overhang. In the meantime the lighthouse station sent out a boat and retrieved the other. They were lucky, unlike most of the men of the Lord Ashburton, who were lost, desperate and unnoticed in the midwinter nighttime storm. It is no wonder that off-island sailors avoid Grand Manan. We have talked to pleasure yachtsmen who have seen its cliffs and unreliable harbors, but only from a safe distance. Few attempt a landing, in any kind of weather. In the usual kind of weather, in fact, one cannot even see the land. The prevailing south wind from the Atlantic, funneled up between Nova Scotia and New Brunswick, hits the cold air given off by the Bay of Fundy waters, and the collision brings the island's air down to its dew point. The south end, most frequently approached by Maine sailors, faces the Atlantic, and whatever weather comes from the Atlantic it gets, with the result that there is a marked difference in temperature between north and south. The southern end, nearly always fogbound, is colder, wilder and more sparsely populated. As one goes north the sun gets at the land more often, and the spring flowers bloom about two weeks earlier. But over the bay, fog predominates, covering reef, cliff and channel alike, and the yachts go somewhere else. The island fishermen, though —

even the small boatmen — cannot let qualms stop them. Out there in the bay is where the money comes from. They have learned the danger places, they ride the tide and they usually come home.

II.

*O*ur second visit to the west cliffs was by trail to Bradford Cove, near the southern end of the island. It is an easy walk of about two miles, and the contrast between east and west is not as noticeable. You start high, in fields full of strawberries, raspberries and blueberries, sometimes all together. (In the high blueberry season, in August, one can pick over a gallon in an hour and a half.) Gradually the fields merge into forest. It is marshy and there are enormous beeches, probably protected by the impossibility of getting any vehicle through the swamp and over the often-flooded streams. We saw the forest in a rainy season and it was about as wet as it could be and still support trees. Underfoot was mud, deep and clinging, and in some places the trail went through running streams and standing black ponds created by beaver dams. Algae grew on live tree trunks and Spanish moss, almost unknown north of Virginia, hung from branches in the warm protection of swampy hollows.

The ground and some of the trees were spectacularly decorated with mushrooms, replacing the field flowers which cannot exist in the dim wet woodland. They are of the fungi, one of the two great original divisions of plant life. Lacking chlorophyll, they get their essential plant carbohydrate food from other plants: they are destroyers, living off live or dead trees. The deadwood in forests is reduced to humus by fungus activity, and if they live on a wound in a live tree they will eventually bring the tree down.

Some of the mushrooms in the Bradford forest are edible, some not. (They all looked suspicious to me, however: the colors were too bright and the shapes too flamboyant to seem quite reliable.) The members of the *Amanita* genus are probably the most dangerous to eat. The kind we saw have bloodred or orange or yellow thick caps sometimes dotted with raised white spots; their stems are pure white, as are the ribbed undersides of their caps (the gills, which contain the spores); but when you break stem or cap the interior quickly turns dark.

We also saw what we think were the edible *Tylopilus felleus* — mostly small, red-capped and red-stemmed mushrooms, except for one that was eight inches across, nearly flat, smooth and yellow-brown, with a deceptively sinister look to it.

A fragrant mushroom, which grew there in quantity, is the

chanterelle, egg-yellow, with a smooth cap upturned and wavy at the edges and long gills descending down the stem almost to earth. These we were safe in picking, and we brought back a basket of them, to be cooked, slowly, with butter, salt and pepper, in a frying pan. A relative of the chanterelle also grows in that wood: the "trumpet of death," so called because it resembles a large, dark funnel. Despite its title it is edible, and is sometimes called horn of plenty.

On one of the old beeches, high up, was a crowded cluster of bright yellow mushrooms, their stems, about five or six inches long, arching upward. This was *Collybia,* which prefers live hardwoods, attacking the wounds where branches had broken off. Though lumbermen had left these trees standing, perforce, they were probably doomed and eventually would fall as the hard old wood that provides support gave way to the attacks of *Collybia* and other fungi.

One odd-looking mushroom, *Suillus granulatus,* is edible and choice. You would only have to close your eyes while eating. The cap is sticky or furry, and dull gray-brown, the underside a fearful yellow-green. Another little mushroom, one of the daintiest, is a member of the Mycena family. It has an attractive down-turned bell-shaped cap with a peak on top, almost like an inch-wide hat, and a very thin stem. It looked like a minuscule man. Could it be that here is one of the origins of the stories of little people that existed concurrently and independently in all temperate-zone countries? A quick look at the large August assemblage of mushrooms in a dark forest, their bright caps hiding their straight stems, and a child's imagination might see them as something both more and less than human. There are the good ones and the bad ones. Our little bell-hatted Mycena is a good one. You can eat it, but it hardly provides a meal, even in quantity.

In my childhood I saw fairy rings in the Maine woods. I think, at nine, I did not believe in fairies, elves, trolls, leprechauns or any of their relations, but I didn't know what had caused the rings. They had a magical look, as if they had been arranged by hand — whose hand? Fairy rings have a natural explanation. If a mushroom's spawn (a mass of threads that takes the place of a root) lives in a place where its food is evenly distributed through the surrounding soil, it will grow out neatly in all directions from where the original spore fell, using up the soil's nutrients as it goes, so that eventually a circle of mushrooms will grow around the original spot. Some of the circles are said to be as much as four hundred years old. An aged fairy ring might have attracted a certain amount of superstition in eras more inclined to magic and mysticism than ours.

Puffballs, the most sophisticated of mushrooms, having all their spores inside their fat round fruiting bodies, were to be found here and there, sometimes the size of a Ping-Pong ball, sometimes just pushing out of the ground, making the earth look like an ant heap with a hard core of whiteness in the center. They are delicious, but there were not enough to collect.

We were familiar with only one of the many lichens of the woods. That is scarlet-crested cladonia, called British soldiers. It grows like hard little old trees on pieces of fallen spruce bark. The gray woody stems are capped by bright red crooked caps. Lichens are a curious combination of fungi and algae. The fungus provides support and water for the alga and the alga provides food for the fungus, both living in mutually dependent relationship. This sturdy small growth looked as if nothing could destroy it, and the scarlet caps shone on the dark ground.

Besides the quantities of fungi there was one flowering plant in these woods, Indian pipe, which does not need sunlight and does not make chlorophyll, but has a blossom, leaves, stem and roots, all white. It was there in all stages, from new plants emerging, their heads pale against the black earth, to tall stems with nodding white flowers, five-petaled, semi-transparent, to the final erect fruit, blackening at the tip. Indian pipe thrives on dead or decaying matter, which provides essential carbohydrates. All plants need carbohydrates, and most need sun and chlorophyll in order to metabolize them. Indian pipe is an anomaly, a real flowering plant, not a mushroom, and it populates dank, damp forests with ghostly elegance. But it contains stamens with yellow anthers, invisible unless one turns one up, and despite its corpselike appearance the blossoms have nectar. Bees fly in and out as if they were invading the homeliest of field flowers.

We seemed to be walking underground, the wood was so dark and the ground like the floor of a cave. Then we came out on fields again, and before us was the sea, at the bottom of tall cliffs. Bradford Cove is a misleading name: it is the barest indentation in the rock wall, with a narrow cobble beach. However it has a small place in Grand Manan's history. In 1807 a German farmer, a fisherman from Seal Cove, and a local doctor agreed to make a settlement there, "for which the Doctor agreed to give us one barrel of pork, a barrel of rum and two barrels of flour and to help us build a home . . ." The supplies lasted a year, which is most surprising. Undoubtedly they got refills from time to time. But they gave up, and the Bradford Cove homestead was taken over by another farmer, who planted grain. There was some desultory interest in establishing a harbor there, a way station for voyages between southern Grand Manan and Maine ports. Since there really was no harbor the project fell through and was quickly forgotten.

Now it is a peaceful, lonely place, with neither road, house, dock or boats. Terns dived and skimmed over blue white-touched water. Since they had lost their nests in a thunder-storm on Machias Seal Island we assumed they were just wandering. Terns are magnificent rovers, and will fly many miles for food, or perhaps just for the pleasure of flying. But possibly, we hoped, they were trying to reestablish a colony on Grand Manan in the face of herring gull competition.

12.

The Whistle, now named Long Eddy Light, is at the northern end of the west cliffs. It was originally only a foghorn, set
on a small house on the rock beach at the edge of the sea. The
keeper had access by a steep set of switchback stairs. The need
for a light was recognized only recently, and a new house was
built on top of the cliff, some three hundred feet up from the
beach. The old Whistle house burned down and the remains
vanished, the sea taking the planks and depositing them elsewhere. The steps are still more or less intact, and we de-

scended on splintered boards. Though the ruins of the old house are no longer there, water has replaced them with weird and beautiful driftwood, scattered plentifully among the pieces of cliff which make up the skimpy beach.

The Whistle at Long Eddy Point is the only lighthouse on the whole length of the west cliffs, down to Southwest Head Light at the other end. Apparently no one is expected to approach Grand Manan that way, and seeing it as we did later, we had no doubt that mariners would either turn back or go around, steering a far course, to anchor in the calm east coast harbors.

The new building looks out to The Wolves, a small group of islands with a lighthouse twelve miles north, and Quoddy Head, Maine, seven miles west. The light — a five hundred-watt bulb that costs five dollars and lasts three months with care (they don't turn it on and off too often) — is backed by a ten-inch reflector, and its beam reaches as far as Blacks Harbour, eighteen miles away. The keeper turns it on one hour before sunset and off one hour after sunrise, and in fog it is on all the time the whistle blows. The foghorn, an especially piercing one right below the light, facing west, is turned on by the keeper when he can't see Quoddy Head or The Wolves. In July it had sounded 620 hours (though even that was not as much as the horn at Machias Seal, which had gone all day, every day of that month). One of the two keepers who has night duty has a cot two stories down, directly below the whistle. He can sleep when it is going, he says. The noise, however, nearly knocked us off the stairs climbing up to the light. The keeper wakes up if the sound stops, knowing the silence means something wrong.

The building is modern, concrete, functional, with three motors and a variety of buttons and switches to control this and that. But nothing is really automatic. A keeper has to be there to turn the switches off and on, and he has to keep a log, in longhand, signed by him, of every hour of his duty. If the current goes off even for less than a second, as it did during the thunderstorm that drowned the tern chicks, he enters it in the log, with the duration of the lapse. He has to watch the clock to turn on the light and watch the sea to turn on the whistle. Whoever designed the building forgot to add screens. As all the lights are on all night and all the windows must always be open, every mosquito within miles converges on the keeper. Another discomfort factor is the noise of the wind in the ventilators around the light, which, especially in winter, can be almost as noisy as the sound of the whistle. The keeper can sleep through that, too. He is proud of his shining house, with all its mosquitoes, noise and light. Nothing really disturbs him except loneliness, and he will keep a visitor with him as long as he can.

South from the Whistle along the west coast there are a few houses, then nothing, no trail, no road. Once there had been a trail, marked with blue paint that now showed indistinctly. We followed it until it became hopelessly overgrown. Pushing through the undergrowth we reached the edge of the cliff and looked southward. There was a scene to dream of. A small pebble beach was bounded by an immense headland, trees dense all over its top, its face to the sea sheered off abruptly. The sky darkened as it had at Eel Falls and often does suddenly for a few minutes, and fog flew in from the sea. So I have always imagined the mountainous country of the Nibelungs, the "land of continual mist" of the Icelandic Sagas, where Sigurd met treachery and death. Grand Manan here again seemed no place of modern history, but a mythical island once found and never more, for which travelers search forever, hoping, led on by old stories.

The fog lifted, and out to sea, about a quarter of a mile

away, we glimpsed a group of little gray and white birds, whirling in the water, sometimes rising and circling together like sandpipers. They were northern phalaropes, seldom seen, as they come to land only to nest in the Arctic and subarctic. There the female, larger and brighter than her mate, pursues him, captures him and chooses the nesting site, reversing the usual procedure. In fact all this lady of leisure does is lay the eggs, once her mate has built the nest by himself. Then she drifts off to a group of her companions, leaving him to incubate the eggs and guard the young. They all migrate southward in August, and as many as 250,000 have been seen to gather in the Bay of Fundy, usually well out of sight of land, to rest and stir up the surface of the water to get at the tiny marine life on which they feed. They cannot dive, being extremely light. On the water they hold their heads high, except when eating, as the breast feathers are thick and buoyant. The phalaropes we saw, numbering perhaps two hundred, had a graceful, proud look, only dipping their bills into the water briefly for food. They are pelagic birds — actually living on the open sea — and no one knows what part of the South Atlantic they inhabit during the winter. To most they are strangers. What a great world of birds exists outside our knowledge, living their lives in solitude or in colonies, breeding in the inaccessible Arctic, swarming all over the oceans. It has been estimated that there are about 100 billion birds. The earth's human population is four billion.

The west cliffs have one real harbor, an extraordinary fjordlike inlet, Dark Harbour, extending narrowly almost a mile inland. It is the only break in the fifteen-mile rock wall. As early as 1803 a settler moved to the harbor, and by the mid-nineteenth century the provincial government considered a development that would make it the major port for

*Dark Harbour, a fjord-
like inlet, is the only bay
on the west coast. Shad-
owed by cliffs, it is always
lightless. A natural dike
of rocks closes it from
the sea.*

the island. The idea never matured, though roads were built and the lumber industry in that area was brisk, taking all the good hardwoods. Dark Harbour has one flaw which is difficult to overcome: waves and cliff detritus have formed a natural breakwater, a great pile of rocks a mile long, and the harbor is completely closed in. Several times government enterprises have undertaken to break through this barrier in different places. It always closes up again. The latest break is at the north end of the beach, close to the shore. The rocks are shored up with heavy planks, and the tide rushes through like a flash flood. Cliff debris must be cleared out continually if the artificial breakthrough is to be maintained. Though it never became the busy port that was envisaged there is some modest industry, dulse gathering and brush weir fishing, and it is a down-at-heels summer resort.

The dusty road to Dark Harbour from the east coast is crossed by ancient lumber roads. There are few habitations, and the young forest is so thick you can't see through it: birch, spruce, larch, and the ever-present alder that fills up any leftover space. There are not many mammals left on the island, and the few that remain are doomed. But on the road to Dark Harbour, where an animal has a fair chance of being unmolested, we saw a white-tailed deer. It stood quietly in the road looking at us, not surprised. It didn't seem to know what to do, and finally turned and walked in front of our car, until it decided to melt back into the dense woods. There it stood and watched us from the shadows. We stopped the car and looked straight into its large eyes until eventually they too disappeared. Able to retreat into a forest where they cannot possibly be seen, one would think the deer would have multiplied. The reverse is true, hunters being stubborn and deer not always so sensible. They had been introduced in

1845, killed off, then replaced — once after the Confederation, again after the First World War, then in 1935 and for several years afterward. In spite of this there are only a few left. Other animals have been introduced — Grand Manan had little animal life before man brought it. In 1784 moose were introduced by Moses Gerrish, one of the early settlers, but they didn't last long. There used to be beaver, otter, muskrat, raccoon, which eats birds' eggs, and gray fox, which eats birds. But hunting is one of the islanders' rare relaxations. Those few animals that have survived the hunters choose inaccessible places.

The Dark Harbour road, which had been rising slowly, now made an abrupt descent. About three hundred feet below was the narrow head of the inlet, carved through rock by Dark Harbour Brook, an insignificant but effective stream hidden by trees. Heavy shade lies over the whole inlet. Its name is apt. Dark Harbour is remarkably lightless. The road down into it is rough, hewn from the cliff wall, and not wide enough for another car to pass. Rocks lie at the edge, sometimes in the middle. We crept in low gear as far down the steep road as we dared. The road widened to admit the parking of two or three cars, and we walked the rest of the way, then turned inland to go around the head of the harbor. Under the trees, where Dark Harbour Brook meanders feebly down from the hill, there were three recently hatched spotted sandpipers, downy and beach-colored. They teetered expertly, in the manner of their parents, their downy tails so small and soft that they undulated like little feather dusters. When they saw us they fled to safety, probably a nearby nest in a thicket.

We continued beyond the brook to the natural outer breakwater, which is high and solid enough to bear shacks. Old fishnets are spread over the rocks, spread with drying dulse. Islanders with summer houses at Dark Harbour spend weekends on both inner and outer beaches. "Summer house" is a euphemism. They are almost all one-room tar-papered shacks. The settlement is the only one on the island that does not visibly express Grand Manan's wealth, unless one can regard owning a weekend hut as evidence of wealth. Most of the inhabitants have rowboats, a few with outboard motors, and an hour before low water they cross the inlet, where the man of the family attaches the boat to a winch at the top of the cobble beach, cranks it noisily to a start with some difficulty, while his family help push the boat up. From the peak they all push it down to the ocean over pebbles stained with boat paint, and take off. They wear fisherman's tall rubber boots, and the idea is to go where someone else has not been recently, get out of the boat and gather the seaweed.

Dulse is a red alga. Most red algae shun sunlight, usually being found in deep water down to two hundred fathoms or more. But dulse is among the few hardy species that can survive in the intertidal zone, and even so it is never found out of the sea, but must be plucked in shallow water when low tide briefly exposes it, not to sun but to light. It has thin dull red fronds, deeply indented, like chicory. Minute leaflets attached along the edges make it look like old wet rags. It is said to be delicious when dried. This is a matter of opinion. Islanders love it. Off-islanders, even if they have lived on Grand Manan twenty years or more, generally find it awful. It is supposed to be very good for you. The only time I liked it was when we had forgotten a piece on the dashboard. The sun had shone on it for several hours and it had become wonderfully crisp. It had all of the sea in its taste. Most dulse, however, is not eaten by the islanders but shipped to the mainland to be converted to a powder full of minerals and vitamins, for pharmaceutical purposes. (Packets of dried dulse can also be found in some mainland supermarkets.)

We stayed for a while on the outer beach, watching the dulse gatherers process their crop, a fairly primitive procedure. When the boats come back their owners load the seaweed into crates and take it to a box with rusty spikes and another hand-cranked motor, to shake it up and separate the fronds, which always stick together around the holdfast. Some simply shake it in a box by hand. Then it is spread over old weir nets on the rocks, and if the weather is good and the low tide has been early, it might be dried in a day. If conditions are not fine, and they usually are not, it is taken into the shacks, to be spread out again the next day.

We waited just too long. It is almost a mile back around the inlet, and the tide was coming up so rapidly that in a few minutes there was nothing between water and impenetrable thicket. Off came our shoes, and we waded over the worst terrain to be imagined. All of Dark Harbour inlet is of rock, and the rock brought down from the cliffs is new and sharp, untamed yet by water. It was like treading on glass. After an hour or so of this we reached the inner beach, which is never quite covered by tide, and walked north to the inlet along wet cobbles.

Water constantly drips from the cliffs above. Some of it is collected into homemade wooden chutes and constitutes the residents' water supply, but mostly it just seeps over the beach, which is already slippery with green algae. The huts, made roughly by hand out of any available cheap material, stand barely above high tide line. Near the northern end of the beach, in an advantageous spot for luring herrings, is a neglected weir. There had been, in the middle of the harbor, a

*Weekend retreats at Dark Harbour are tar-papered shacks.
Their owners cross the landlocked bay to gather dulse in
the sea outside at low tide.*

carefully tended weir, but no one got herring from it. We had twice watched a seining there. The first time the net came up empty, the second time it contained four herrings. The crew was too slow pulling in the purse net, and the fish escaped out of the open bottom. The fact is that the Dark Harbour people seem somewhat on the shiftless side, unlike the hard-working fishermen of the east coast. Now the good weir is gone, poles and all, and only the ragged one by the inner beach is left. Seaweed hangs from torn netting like old clothing and the poles lean toward each other. Its owner, a young weekender, keeps meaning to mend it, but intentions are all he has. An osprey hangs over the harbor, feeding on the herring that the tide brings in. For him it is good fishing.

The only thing well kept up is the man-made inlet. It looks strong enough to withstand the worst battering by tide, but there is no doubt it will give way eventually, as the others have. We walked a catwalk. Below us the tide was tearing in on a slant, dark-waved, compelled by the narrow way into the speed of a mountain river. The young herrings come with it, forced by the heavy flow. Bright yellow strings of toggles stream in a semicircle around the inner entrance. The fish go past them because they can do nothing else, but they are too frightened by the dancing floats to go back out again until the tide takes them, and even then the young fish hang back if they can, secure in the deep inner water. That harbor must be thick with herring. Along the inlet, on the bottom, the fronds of long-stalked laminaria look like great fish, each swimming eternally in one place. It is the same kind of plant I had picked up, torn from its moorings, on the eastern beach. The Dark Harbour people don't bother to gather it, but it is a useful plant. In manufacture it is burned; the ashes separated into their different mineral constituents and used for medicinal purposes. Mainly it is a source of iodine. Waving there in the racing water it looks too alive ever to be pulled up and burned. It is safe. Dark Harbour doesn't care. Dulse is the main concern, and apparently all the gathering, a process so simple that many children make several hundred dollars each summer, makes hardly a dent in the supply.

13.

*O*ur fifth adventure with the west cliffs was unintended. Grand Manan is old, as geology goes. It goes back before the ice age, almost to the beginning of the earth's crust. On the east coast you can see its age — the tidal estuaries; the one-time mountains that are now low-lying islands, the highest seventy-four feet; the basaltic sand that was once molten rock on a new planet. The Bay of Fundy, once a valley, is as old as its mountains. But the west cliffs seem to be a different country, starting with a ridge that runs the length of the island. That section, a mere 160 to 185 million years old, is young compared to the elderly, sunken eastern side. It is, in fact, one long mountain range, from Southwest Head to the Whistle. Eel Lake lies low on its summit, and is thought to be the crater of a volcano, one of several along the high center ridge. West, south and north the forest rises above it, and the lake is a deep-set, gleaming eye seen first from far above through dark spruces.

We had followed the course of Eel Brook from the eastern beach where it emptied, up to the strange little falls. Now we wanted to trace it to its source, Eel Lake. A two-rutted, grass-grown lane led straight to the lake and to the two well-kept cabins on it. That was an easy walk, say, for a rainy day. But a trail led away from the lake, well-marked at first; it was used originally by families who lived on fishing and dulse collecting on Indian Beach on the west coast. The more carefully protected island children were afraid of them, "wild men," they thought, like gypsies.

We soon found that neither wild men nor trail existed any more. Curiosity drove us on, led by the much faded blue marks hidden behind ferns and low-growing alders. The island had suffered from the long drought that afflicted the whole eastern Atlantic coast, but the generous abundance of ferns proved that it is a wet place anyway. The normal annual rainfall is over fifty inches, and even in dry summers fog protects its plant life. One of the few remaining beavers had a dam and a house in the woods, and water lurked there whatever the weather. It was open water, black from the color of the mud just beneath it, and it harbored an abundance of wild calla, an exotic plant that looks cultivated but is not related to the South African calla that grows in greenhouses and appears at funerals. This, also called water arum, was named by Linnaeus from the Greek *kallaia,* a cock's wattles, and exists only in the northern temperate zone. It is a long-stemmed beauty with thin heart-shaped leaves and a large white apparent flower like a hood over the actual small, greenish flower. In the desolate, cut-over woods it gleamed, vigorous and tall and out of place. About a week later the calyxes had turned green, the blossoms had gone to seed and their places taken by thick, bulbous stalks of seedpods. The leaves were yellow and withering. The calla area, that showed so white and virginal above the water, had become a waste.

There were few scented flowers in the woods, but there was scent all around us from the prolific ferns, and once in a while the nostalgic incense of balsams or the sudden, heavy fragrance of meadowsweet.

Wherever there was an open space it was filled with ferns. Each of the four species had its own field; they did not mix. The commonest was bracken, a tall fern, up to three feet, with two or three widely spreading fronds on a single stem. Though coarse-looking it can be eaten in spring, when it is young. Another was wood fern, its single frond about two feet high, dark green, rich and heavy. It is one of the few hardy ferns, and is cut for house decorations — overcut, perhaps. Once in a while a field smelled like new hay, from the hay-scented fern, pale green, smaller and delicate, its leaves subdividing until they were as thin as paper. Sensitive fern was the fourth, its side leaves not cut through to the midriff. The fronds arched gracefully. It is not picked, as it wilts quickly. In the wild it is immediately withered by frost.

The age of the fern family is impressive. Not only is it among the earliest land plants, going back some 400 million years, but at one time it was the highest form of plant, its numbers covering a large part of the earth, many as tall as the tallest oak today. When the tree ferns declined, as the world was inundated by warm water in the Mississippian epoch of

350 million years ago, their dead forms pressed down into the soft earth and hardened into coal.

Along the brushy path we heard a winter wren sing, and stopped to listen. No sound in the world is so joyous, and few birds are heard so seldom. You have to go a long way, quietly, into a deserted forest, to hear this shy creature. Warbles and trills, brilliant and high-pitched, continued past belief, like the Emperor's Nightingale, until it seemed the bird must have lost breath. We lost ours in listening. The wren sat in the twisted roots of an overturned tree, where it nested, brown, small, almost invisible. It was unimaginable that such a volume of song came from such a little source. Long after we had left its nesting place we heard the song, rippling high and unearthly through the trees, like laughter. Probably the bird was angry at our intrusion. All quarrels would vanish if human anger were as sweet to the ear. We were in an enchanted forest.

Overhead another bird was angry. A thin complaint like the call of the wood peewee came from the top of a dead tree. A broad-winged hawk perched there, small and stout, peering down at us. It did not seem afraid, nor did it attack. Its mate joined it and they stared at us together as if they had never seen such beings. When we moved they flew, keeping near but not obtrusive. They were slow hawks, heavy-built and short-winged, but they maneuvered agilely between the close-set trees, fanning their white-banded tails. The chunky pair were breeding about as far north as the species goes — they are rarely seen on Grand Manan. Yet they seemed entirely at home, almost tame. We could not find the young. Probably, unsure of flight, they hid in the fork of a tree and watched us alertly while we looked for them.

Beyond the broad-winged hawks there came a sudden harsh warning, the repeated calls of a goshawk. This is a bird whose nest we avoided seeking, as it is probably the most ferocious of all birds, a fierce and fearless hunter that will attack humans savagely if the nest is approached. Two of them darted through the tops of the trees, large gray shadows. Though not falcons, they were trained for falconry in medieval times because of their remarkable prowess as hunters. A goshawk has been known to chase a chicken under a woman's skirt, and in the forest it will search low, seeking groundbirds, squirrels or rats in the underbrush. It is the largest of the *Accipiter* genus, long-tailed and short-winged, all known for their hunting abilities. For a long time we heard the warning cries through the woods, then all was silent.

It was time to go home. We had not brought lunch, not knowing the vastness of these woods. But we went on. There was still an occasional blue mark, but the trail was casual. It had probably not been trod for many years. Then the forest changed; it no longer felt enchanted. It diminished to brambles and dwarfed spruces, and the track, almost indistinguishable, descended with startling suddenness. We were going down the western slope of the range, and it was far steeper than the mild eastern incline. Within a few minutes we had slipped and tripped to the bottom, grasping at precariously rooted trees on the way down.

At the bottom there was nothing but sea, and it was preposterous that anyone had troubled to make a trail to it, much less lived there. The map did say Indian Beach, but there was no beach, only mounds of rock, some sharp-edged and splintered, others smoothed by water. Our way down, we saw, was a narrow, precipitous gash in the rock wall that stretched enormously in both directions, and the beach was the waste of this long cliff. The bay was just off high tide, and there was very little, even of rock fall, between us and the waves. To the north was Long Eddy Light, possibly twenty minutes' walk. The caretaker's house was visible, but the cliff thrust into the sea between it and us, blocking it from access. Southward was another headland, where a large section of cliff had fallen. It looked negotiable, and we made for it. On the other side were houses, and there was sure to be a road. But the houses were closed shacks with tar paper at the windows. Near them were piles of faded lobster pots, and we guessed that from here some of the lobstermen went out in winter to set their traps. Not only was there no road, but the cliff leaned outward, its middle gouged out by a rockslide. It was evident that the only road to these houses was by sea, and, judging from the deteriorated state of the precipice, it was often a rough sea, undermining the rock wall and dragging large pieces of it underwater.

A boat was distantly visible. We went to the point and waved, and in a few minutes the boat was near enough for us to identify a single man, rowing. He strained against the pull of the falling tide, an old man, very thin, and we wished we had not waved him in. But there he was, and we helped him pull his boat up on the rocks. Without question he took us on board, and was climbing in himself when the boat was sucked out to sea again and began to make its way northward with marvelous rapidity. The old man seized his oars and forced the boat round to the south. He had hit a powerful current just offshore, and this, combined with the drag of the ebb tide, made the boat nearly unmanageable.

But he coped. He rowed facing forward, as do all fishermen, to distinguish submerged rocks; and from my perch in the stern I could see the cords of his back muscles as he slowly defeated the sea. He was going, he told us, just a short way, to his own winter shack, to clean his lobster pots and put them away for the summer. He had come a long distance, from far around the northern point, rowing for three and a half hours against current, wave and tide, and he would have to go back the same way. No, there was no road, he said, not anywhere along here until Dark Harbour, which was a good piece beyond his stop. We could walk it easily, he added, but must mind the cliff. It falls down. He would not be rowing if he had money to buy a motor. His old one had given out some years back, and just after, his boat had cracked up on the rocks in a storm. It had taken all he had to get a new one. Even so, with the high price of lobster, he might have made enough, but he had few pots. His wife had been hit by a drunken driver and left with both legs paralyzed. Of his seven children, all were married and gone away but one girl, who had had polio when she was a baby and was still home, and paralyzed too. Now, in the summer, he fished for pollock with a handline. He had not caught any fish at all last week. This sorrowful tale was told in bits, with the greatest good humor, as he picked his way along the treacherous shoreline, keeping close to avoid the north-bearing current, steering around water-covered rocks with the frontward rowing which looked clumsy but was dexterous. He said he was sixty-four but he looked ten years older, worn out with work. One of his sons should be helping him, we said. Why should they, he answered; they have their own children to look after, and it isn't easy for any small fisherman hereabouts. His story might have been vintage soap opera but was not. He asked for no pity; he was matter-of-fact and liked to talk. This was not one of the old "wild men" of the west coast, just an unfortunate who attracted bad luck.

He drew into his own beach, again fighting the quickly falling tide, and let us off there, on the wet rocks. We pulled his boat up with him and said good-bye. He shook hands with each of us and warned us again to watch the cliff. He was terribly sad, to us, the more so for being genial.

We studied the map again. He had rowed us less than half a mile, and Dark Harbour looked to be about three miles on. In spite of the hour, about the middle of the afternoon, we were optimistic, infused with the spirit of the old fisherman. However he had not given us a hint of the dilapidated state of the west coast. The three miles stretched to nearer five, and took over three hours, without rest. There was never a place to put the foot down naturally. The cliff's litter defeated us on both sides. The smooth waterside stones were covered with fine seaweed and slippery as glass. Toward the cliff were rock splinters which cut through our thin-soled sneakers. Above that were large boulders that we climbed over, using hands, feet, sometimes rumps, as we were too tired to be dignified. Once in a while a real sand beach beckoned like a mirage. It always was a mirage. There was no sand, but a flat surface of small round stones that slithered under our feet. It was like walking on billiard balls, and we turned with relief to the debris farther up.

Sometimes we watched the cliff, as counseled. It varied from three hundred to four hundred feet, majestic and dangerous. Where it hadn't been eroded by storm action it rose in straight columns divided by enormous squarish blocks with an architectural appearance. The name of this kind of rock is trap, from the Swedish *trappa,* meaning stair, and it was once the flow of lava, fairly young in geology. The uneasy rock, sharp-edged and ready to fall, looked young, but it didn't seem possible that it had ever flowed.

The loneliness was appalling and beautiful. Since we had left the fisherman's hut there had not been another habitation. There was no room for one. The cliff dropped almost straight into the sea, with only the narrow edge of rock fall for us to walk on. In a storm or fog, or at high tide, we wouldn't have been able to move at all. But then we would not have tried. We were lucky. Bruised feet and parched throats were nothing against the magnificent desolation of rock wall dropping forever, it seemed, into burning bright sea. It is, of course, possible to visit the west cliffs by boat, but that way one only sees it. We experienced it.

At last we saw houses again, and the deep indentation of Dark Harbour. There was something better for us at Dark Harbour than herring and dulse: fresh cold water springing out of the rock. We bathed burning faces and drank, and it was the coldest, freshest water in the world.

There were two men there, and they seemed the best men in the world, because they had a car, and were about to drive across the island. We were strange apparitions, coming from the cliff. No one, they believed, ever walked along the west coast. But they took us in without comment and immediately offered us rum and dulse. The rum we refused, but we accepted a small amount of dulse. It was dry as autumn leaves, and very tough. We chewed for half an hour, until they dropped us at the main road, and we still had not swallowed it. The men ate it by the handful, like popcorn.

The road from Dark Harbour was entirely devoid of people. We met only one car, going the other way, and saw no houses. The forest was far more monotonous than the cliff. It would have been a long, dull haul homeward on foot, and we would not have made civilized Grand Manan before night.

A very thin strip it is, where fishermen and children and churches have established their foothold. Grand Manan is lonely and dangerous and beautiful, and largely uninhabitable. It has not changed much since the Indians precariously

South from the Whistle, on the west wall, is a cobble beach bounded by a headland of impenetrable forest. The island's mountainous west side is empty of people, as it has always been.

visited it and Champlain found it so daunting that he did not try to land, and the early puritan settlers found their new life unexpectedly hard even for them. Grand Manan, on the whole, still belongs to itself.

Island of Shells

Sanibel

I.

*O*ff the Gulf coast of Florida, less than three degrees from the Tropic of Cancer, is an island deceptively gentle, decked with coconut palms, mangrove forests and shell-crusted beaches. Sanibel Island is about eleven miles long and two and a half at its widest. Unlike the other islands in its archipelago Sanibel's position is east and west, and the northward-moving Gulf Stream blesses its southern shore with the profusion of shells that has made it famous, as well as the damp

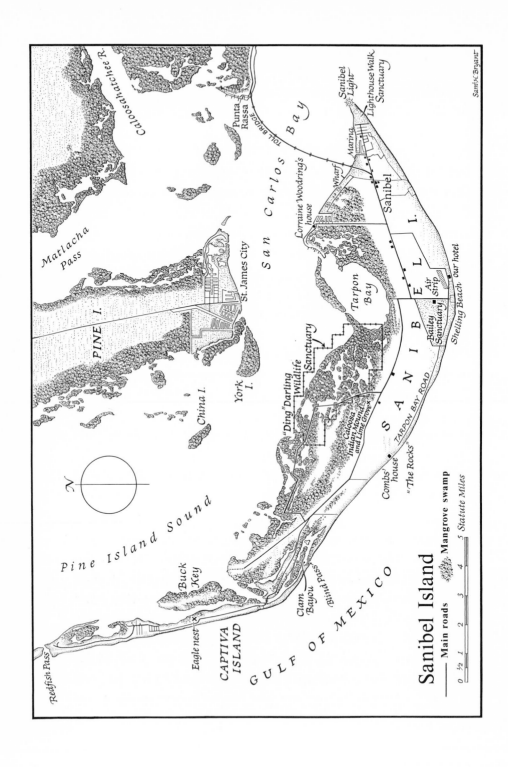

Sanibel Island

— Main roads   Mangrove swamp

0 ½ 1 2 3 4 5 Statute Miles

Sam H. Bryant

south wind that blows mosquitoes off the beach and quiets the fierceness of the subtropical sun.

Sanibel's east-west position takes the full force of storms from the south, as well as the Gulf Stream. All along the southern coast are ancient shell ridges, and the island grows constantly, built by storm action on the south and by mangrove forest on the north. It has been rising ever since the first tilting that brought Sanibel into being, but it hasn't gotten very far. Fourteen feet above sea level is its highest. As an island it could not have been very impressive in the beginning, with tides and winds rolling its bleached sands from one side to the other, and no living creature to be seen. Then the sea brought mangrove seedlings and coconuts, and birds flying over dropped seeds of other plants that can grow in sand, and the desolate little piece of ocean bottom became a garden.

On the island's north side, facing Pine Island Sound, mangroves have control. The low dark green forest has grown, and continues to grow, over the quiet water of the Sound, enclosing bays and inlets and creating lagoons and swamps. This motionless place is home for millions of baby shrimps and the fingerlings of most of the Gulf fishes. It is also the winter or all year round refuge for hosts of marsh and bay birds, who eat the shrimp and the fingerlings and roost on the short thick-growing trees.

Sanibel is known to have been inhabited by humans for about thirty-five hundred years, though its residents, until the last decade of the nineteenth century, have left small trace. It may have been lived on far longer. No one knows who were the first people, before the Caloosa Indians, except that there were people. Everything about the island favors human habitation. The Caloosas came from the Caribbean and South America, and have been traced on the island as far back as two thousand years before the first Spanish Conquistador set

Mangroves grow in the quiet water of Sanibel's north side. The island is getting bigger all the time as the low dark forest spreads.

his doomed foot on Florida's Gulf coast. It was a Spanish invader who named the Caloosas for posterity. They were primarily fishermen, so they preferred living on islands or coasts, only penetrating the treacherous interior marsh on hunting trips for a change of diet. Their towns were near the water, and they built them well. The most notable feature was a pyramid-shaped hill of shells thirty to forty feet above the near sea level lands they occupied: a sensible precaution (not taken by the present inhabitants) against abnormally high equinoctial tides. About twenty dwelling places were placed among shell-built steps and terraces, and a wide ramp led to the top, the home of the chief and his family alongside the temple and the storehouses. It is not known what the Caloosas' houses looked like, as only foundations remain: low mounds with the traces of formal terraces, steps and ramps, and canals. For their boats they built slips protected by shell jetties which opened out to sea. There were gardens with shell borders. Each town had a canal which led to an artificial lake in the center of which was another pyramid of shells, a burial mound, smaller than the hills of the living. A ramp spiraled to the flat-topped summit, which was probably both a temple and a city of the dead. On Sanibel human bones were found in the traces of such a burial mound, and a causeway leading to the chief's dwelling, where there are still potsherds.

The shells the Caloosas used were the common ones of the region. The pyramids were faced with conchs in a swirling mosaic. The same shells lined the side walls, and the ramps and causeways were paved with large surf clams. The foundations of the walls were conchs driven into the ground, narrow points first, like fat nails. Then shell fragments were added and the foundation solidified with marl, the island's clay. These were not primitive savages. From their southern origins they had brought a civilization, simple but adequate.

While no houses remain, they must have built them low and sturdy, to withstand the force of the wind. For although Sanibel's wind usually seems as mild as a spring breeze, that breeze can alter in an hour, turning the island into a tearing waste of uprooted trees, windowless, roofless houses and gardens many feet deep in water and ocean-bottom sand.

In their high-held temples the Caloosas worshiped the sun, a practice which continues among their present-day successors. In daily living they were resourceful, using every material that came to hand. They made floats for fishing, of the native gumbo-limbo wood, lashed with gut sinews; the fish hooks were of thin, tough twigs; the lines were of Spanish moss, twisted into thread. For larger fish they cut and stretched thongs of deer hide or wove strong fibers of yucca; the nets were of interlaced palmetto leaves. The biggest fish were harpooned with a spear carved of bone.

The Caloosa families were called by the Spanish the *pescadores grandes*. This referred not only to the skill of Caloosa fishermen — and perhaps to their physical size — but to the rich fisheries. In spring and fall were the great catches of kingfish, mackerel and mullet in migration, the schools so large the mild Gulf was torn up as if a hurricane had struck, its waters roiled with the splashing and slicing of fins and the surfacing of hundreds of thousands of fish. The catch was salted, smoked or sun-dried and the roe was carefully preserved separately.

The Indians were also agricultural, raising corn, pumpkins, squash and tobacco in their shell-bordered gardens. Sometimes they went inland to hunt for deer, bear, turkey, opossum, even rattlesnake, which they preserved in the same ways as they did the fish. Much that grew wild was good to eat: sea grapes, papaya, prickly pear fruit, hearts of palm from the palmetto, coconut. An unending source of food was provided by the millions of mollusks that the south wind brought on shore and the small sweet oysters that roosted on mangrove stems. Sea turtles were then plentiful, and were speared as they came up to breathe. An *outré* item of diet was the breast of a young girl which (it is said but not authenticated) was given to the chief after a successful intertribal raid.

They were not a peaceful people. They used their land well and defended it fiercely. In appearance they were tall, clean-cut and light brown. Another foot of height was added by a fiber structure worn on the head, with the hair wound around it. Bernal Díaz wrote that they looked like giants, and skeletons prove that he did not exaggerate. One male skeleton found was seven feet long, another eight. To de Soto, whom they greeted with unanimous dislike, they also seemed enormous, and from their tall bows "they discharged arrows with such force as to penetrate armor at the distance of two hundred yards." But the Spanish were not too harried to observe the women, handsome and straight, wearing short skirts of closely woven Spanish moss that looked like fine wool.

The Caloosas traded regularly with Caribs, Arawaks and other Indians of the Caribbean Islands and Central America, less often with the Mayans and Aztecs of Mexico. They traveled in canoes of hollowed trees, which they lashed together into catamarans and propelled by paddles and sails made of the ever-useful palmetto which covered the island. From their Indian cousins to the south the Caloosas first learned of the exceptional cruelty of the conquering Spaniards, whose chief desires were gold and slaves. Those Indians the Spaniards could not succeed in enslaving they killed. Castilian gentlemen used to find it a sport to shoot Indians. They would count it a bad day if they did not bag twelve, one for each apostle. Twelve years after the discovery of Haiti and Puerto

Rico, the Spanish had managed to kill in one way or another nearly a million Indians of these two islands. The Caloosas knew the islands well from trading, and many refugees fled to Florida to escape annihilation and to warn of the terrible invaders.

Therefore the Florida Indians greeted the Conquistadores, traveling ever northward in search of booty to enrich their estates and finance more expeditions, with hostility. In the beginning, before the Caloosas were weakened by the combination of promised bribes and mayhem, they killed every Spaniard they could sight through the feathers of their long strong arrows, or pierce with the decorated stilettos they made from the foreleg bones of deer, or brain with an *atlatl,* an Aztec throwing club.

Amerigo Vespucci was a secret adventurer. He went four times to the New World, on the instigation of Ferdinand II of Aragon and without the knowledge of Queen Isabella. He was in business with the king, and the queen was not notified. The business was the bringing back of Indian slaves. This was good for their souls, thought Ferdinand, in addition to being good for his purse. Isabella would not have agreed, so Vespucci's four voyages were kept quiet. In 1498 Vespucci, having journeyed to Honduras, went to Yucatan, crossed the Gulf and circumnavigated its north shore. In April of that year he sailed south the entire length of the Florida Gulf coast, then north on the Atlantic coast, capturing two hundred Indians in the course of trading and fighting. He repeated these exploits three more times in different parts of the Americas, always without publicity. Oddly, the only man who openly recognized Vespucci's expeditions was Columbus (who never took slaves). When Columbus was aging and poor, after the death of his queen, he went to Vespucci and begged him to "tell them what you have seen and what I have seen," and for some months the more successful adventurer pleaded with the king for aid to the ailing, disappointed admiral.

Because of the secret nature of Vespucci's enterprises the southern peninsula of Florida, the Gulf coast and islands were mapped before they were explored officially. The Cantino map of 1502, giving evidence of careful examination of both coasts, was drawn, some think, by Vespucci or someone who accompanied him. Others contend that it was made by the pilot of John Cabot, the ubiquitous Italian, who happened to be down that way the same time Vespucci was. Another map, made in 1508, showed Florida's outline in detail, and in 1510 the Spanish government claimed Florida through the rights of discovery.

Ponce de León's famous voyage in 1513 was obviously not a first. A number of quaint superstitions had grown up before Ponce made his landings. The Indians had tails, there were mermaids in the calm inlets (probably female manatees, those sluggish sea mammals that live in lagoons and quiet river mouths and grow sizable breasts when their young are nursing), and there was a fountain from whose bright water one could recapture youth. These and other legends circulated in Europe among a gullible population much like that which reads today's more sensational tabloids. In the West Indies the tales aroused only cynicism and laughter. Ponce de León, at the time a resident of Cuba, asked for and received a deed from Ferdinand to explore Florida. There he sought slaves, gold, spices and rare woods, of which the king was to receive ten percent. An old hand in the West Indies, Ponce was certainly not looking for a fountain which, however miraculous, would not have enriched him. In fact the water he encountered all over the peninsula was then, as now, brackish, ill-tasting and colored by algae.

In spite of himself, during the search for gold which did not exist and slaves who would not be enslaved, Ponce made one great discovery. He did not know what it was, but he noted it for posterity. It was the Gulf Stream, "the great ocean river," faster than the Mississippi or the Amazon, which flows through the Florida Straits at nearly five miles an hour.

Ponce planted the flag of Spain on the east coast, about eighteen miles north of the later site of St. Augustine, then sailed his three boats, carrying only fighters and sailors, with no excess baggage in the form of priests or doctors, around the southern end where he found islands populated by huge turtles. He named the islands the Tortugas, in recognition of their chief inhabitants. On the Gulf coast he found the beautiful long islands and the towering Indian villages of Pine Island Sound, and there was his true landfall. He named the loveliest and most habitable of the islands Santa Isabella, after the Queen of Aragon, who had died in 1504. In time the name was corrupted to San y Bel, Sennybel and Sanibel, verbal accommodations of Indians and Englishmen to a language they did not understand.

The name of the local Indians Ponce recorded in his journal as Calos. Its meaning is not know, nor if it is an Indian word at all. On his second visit he changed the name slightly, to Carlos, in honor of Charles I, who had succeeded to the throne of Spain after the death of Ferdinand in 1516. (Charles united the kingdom of Spain with the Holy Roman Empire on being elected Emperor Charles V in 1519, and he was the founder of the Hapsburg dynasty.) Whatever the original meaning of the word, it was appropriated wholesale by succeeding Spanish invaders, indiscriminately including Carlos Bay, Carlos River (re-Indianized into Caloosahatchee), the Indian tribes themselves and the various chiefs with whom the Spanish had dealings.

Ponce anchored in the calm water between Sanibel and Punta Rassa on the mainland. In spite of the immediate ferocity of his reception, in the course of which one Indian, probably a refugee from the West Indies, shouted at him in Spanish, the explorer loved this land of palms, wide beaches and lagoons. He succeeded, between fights, in trading for some low-grade gold (the Caloosas were not goldworkers, nor was there any gold to be mined in Florida; they had got the inferior gold in trading with other Indians) and resolved to come back and settle.

Before he could arrange a new expedition several minor Conquistadores succeeded in making the Indians even angrier. The Spanish were better armed than those they would conquer, having crossbows and muskets; but the Indians were expert shots with their longbows, and beat back several invasions. A severe hindrance to the Spanish fighters were their heavy coats of leather and steel armor. The semitropical heat and the constant attention of red bugs, mosquitoes and gnats under these constricting garments added even more to the woes of the invaders than the weapons of the attacked.

Ponce de León had received in 1514 the title Adelantado de La Florida, now known as the Florida Peninsula but then still thought, even by explorers, to be an island. In 1521 he arranged to go back to the bay and the Gulf islands which had so pleased him, and take up his title. King Charles paid lip service to the doctrine of converting the Indians, and Ponce wrote to him: "I return to that island, if it please God's will to settle it . . . that the name of Christ may be praised there, and your Majesty may enjoy the fruit that the land produces." This time some priests went along, as well as the necessary complement of 250 armed men. His two ships carried, in addition, horses, mares, heifers, sheep, goats, hogs and seeds.

The party landed at Punta Rassa, opposite the easternmost point of Sanibel, and began to build houses and a chapel. They didn't get far. An army of Indians arrived in canoes, and one of the powerful arrows, tipped with a fish bone, pierced the leader in the side. Eighty Spaniards were killed, and the would-be colonists gathered up their wounded, hurried back to the ships and departed to Cuba. Nine days later Ponce de Léon died there of his wound.

Ponce had what may be called among the conquerors goodwill. He did not desire, on his second expedition, the death or enslavement of the natives. In this he differed from his successors. Pánfilio de Narváez brought four hundred men to the region in 1529 and tortured what Indians he could catch. He cut off noses and ears and, in bitter excess, threw the chief's wife to his dogs, who ate her alive. He lived to get away, but only four of his men went with him; the other 396 had been killed.

Hernando de Soto tried friendliness in the beginning. He brought to the land of the Caloosas the contents of an entire city with suburbs and farms. Eleven ships carried one thousand men, not counting twenty-four priests and monks and a large number of slaves (the soldiers demanded at least one servant each). There were two hundred and fifty horses, mules, cattle, hogs, six packs of dogs, starch from the nutritious rootstock of cassava, corn, shoulders of bacon, orange and other garden seeds. There was to be a new civilization on the beautiful Gulf coast. Landing on the eastern point of Sanibel, de Soto noted in his journal "a great number of pine trees without tops, standing at the bottom of the Bay, like which there is no spot in the whole extent of this coast." There was also "a singular hummock or grove of pine trees, standing very near the beach, and the only one of its form and kind in all these parts." One wonders what he actually saw. There are no pine trees on Sanibel now. The Australian pine, introduced about sixty years ago, is not a true pine.

De Soto made fast his ships, as had Ponce de León, near Punta Rassa, and a few soldiers went on land in small boats to get grass for the horses. The next day three hundred foot soldiers went ashore and took possession, as they thought, with the usual hopeful device of raising a flag. Flags meant little to the embittered Indians. At the first sign of the invaders they abandoned all their cities, then on the third day reappeared in force without warning and set on the sleeping Spaniards at dawn. De Soto, disheartened, sent his seven largest ships back to Havana, tried to make friends with "Chief Carlos," failed, and moved north, searching for a place worthier of becoming "civilized." His heavily laden men and horses found the going extremely difficult. Food and drinkable water were scarce. At every Indian village they took the products of the storehouses, burned the thatch on the houses and pressed natives into service as guides. One group of guides landed them in a swamp, and de Soto, following precedent, fed four of them to his starved dogs. In this way his miserable company moved north and west, out of Caloosa country, finding "neither gold nor silver nor anything of value."

Without intending it, however, de Soto left in his bloody wake the seeds of Florida's future. Orange pips carelessly dropped grew into trees; escaped cattle multiplied on inland prairies, swine strayed and went wild, thriving in the lush growth at the edges of the swamps.

In the sixteenth century, despite setbacks, Spain still wanted Florida, as a link between her empire to the south and the unknown land to the north. The Spanish claimed that Pope

Alexander had given them everything from Florida to Nova Scotia, and tried to defend that claim for two hundred years. Since the Indians of Florida could not be persuaded by force they should be tamed by Christian faith.

Several missionaries were killed and others departed, disappointed. "Rogel had some corn," reported one Jesuit missionary of another, "which attracted the Indians to him to the extent that they heard the doctrine but when the maize was exhausted their attendance ceased."

But missionaries kept coming until Florida became American in a fuzzy and not strictly legal manner in 1819. Of the effectiveness of the missions a Spanish official stated in 1788 that "since the year 1528 . . . there has never been a single instance of a Florida Indian being genuinely converted and remaining steadfast in the Catholic religion to the day of his death."

The last serious Spanish conqueror was Pedro Menéndez de Avilés, who was responsible for founding St. Augustine in 1565, the first permanent settlement on the North American continent. He then went around the tip, as had many before him, and landed in the now familiar area, poisoned by its history of blood and death but still attractive to explorers from the south. It was not only irresistibly lovely but had the first large protected harbor to be met by ships sailing up the Gulf coast.

Menéndez called on the chief, as usual named Carlos, with a Renaissance show of entertainers, musicians, singers, dancers and a dwarf. His entourage made such an impression that Carlos insisted on giving the explorer, as a reward, the hand of his sister in marriage. Menéndez was already married, but to avoid offending the unusual friendliness of his host, went through a mock ceremony, had the lady baptized Doña Antonia and sent her off to Havana immediately, to be instructed in the Christian faith, incidentally removing her embarrassing presence. The friendship was brief. Menéndez tried in vain to win control of this beautiful shore and its proud people. In 1573 he wrote his king, Philip II, that "the Indians of South Florida are very blood thirsty . . . a menace to the Spanish," and asked permission to "exterminate or enslave them." Instead he himself died and the Caloosas continued to occupy their ancient towns, "more barbarous than ever." Once in a while a brave Spaniard sailed among their islands, not to conquer but to trade. He found little. Bird feathers, smoked fish, fruits and pelts were all the Indians' trading wealth. Even the determined missionaries finally gave up, and in 1747 the Spanish governor of Florida wrote that no one would go to the country of the Caloosas "on account of the horror they feel when they hear the name." But the spirit of the Indians was deteriorating. They were exiled into the interior and orders were given to destroy all their mound cities, to discourage their coming back. They never did.

The experiences of the Conquistadores and the missionaries should have convinced their series of kings that there was nothing to be had in Florida. Its soil was either marshy or sandy, not easily conducive to culture; it had no products to enrich the kingdom of Spain, as had Peru and Mexico; its Indians refused to be friendly and could not be enslaved; the weather was uniformly terrible and the insects worse.

All these conditions still exist with the exception of the Indians. The Caloosas were to be conquered and finally exterminated by the Seminoles in the mid-eighteenth century. The Seminoles in their turn fought new intruders, citizens of the young United States. After twenty years of expensive and frustrating war our government succeeded in removing most of the Seminoles to the West, much against their wishes. The remnants of this mixed race of small, dark, stocky Indians, so different from their tall predecessors, exist today in intimidated groups, selling baskets and small alligators to tourists along the Tamiami Trail.

No civilization that came after the Caloosa was so dignified, so considerate of the land and its creatures. When the Caloosas lived, Sanibel, the other islands and the coast were as nature made them, the Indians using only what was necessary for life. There was no wanton or mercenary destruction of a beautiful heritage.

By the middle of the eighteenth century not an Indian, of any race, remained on Sanibel, where the Caloosas' noble city had faced the dark water of Pine Island Sound. Instead, the island became the temporary abode of pirates. These men had no great stature in the criminal world of the sea. Pirates, to be successful, interested themselves in quick profits, and these could be more easily found among the fat fleets that sailed between Europe and South America, through the Bahamas and the Windward Passage. The Gulf had little to offer, and its pirates were a bedraggled lot who had probably failed in more spectacular areas.

One of the nastiest in this minor league was Henri Caesar, later called Black Caesar. He was a slave in Haiti, the son of a slave woman and an unknown white man. As was customary with part white offspring in that colony, he lived in the house of his master and was trained as a houseboy. He grew very large, over six feet, with huge hands and feet. His size, combined with his stupidity, made him clumsy. He was always dropping things or falling over things. At sixteen he was put out of the house and ordered into the saw yard, where he worked hard, developing enormous strength, and learned to hate the white overseer who whipped him for his dull wits. When Toussaint Louverture led the revolution of the slaves against the French plantation owners, a few years after the

French Revolution, Caesar, not a revolutionary in any other sense, bound the overseer between two planks and sawed him here and there until he died. Having tasted blood he never lost the appetite. He joined the guerrilla blacks, again not on account of revolutionary ardor but for the simpler purpose of pillage and rape. One day he saw a Spanish frigate offshore. He persuaded a few other cutthroats to join him, stole a fishing boat and took the ship with ease, murdering all the crew but the captain and three others. These he needed to show him how to run a vessel, and when they had served their purpose he stabbed them and slung them into the sea. He sailed up the Gulf coast and made his headquarters the destroyed mounds of Sanibel's old Caloosa city on the bay, from which Indians had once paddled out clad only in loincloths, to attack heavily armed Spaniards. Black Caesar, however, fearing battle, attacked only defenseless ships. On short trips to the mainland he raided isolated, unprotected fishing villages. He cannot have made a glorious living, but he was a terror to the fishermen and traders who had to pass through Pine Island Sound. Whoever was captured was killed, sometimes with torture. He was finally captured himself, and burned to death in a fire lit, it is said, by the widow of a preacher whose eyes he had burned out.

Black Caesar was probably typical of the human scum that invaded, for small profit, the islands and mainland colonies of the Gulf coast during the eighteenth century. Mention must be made of one other, Gasparillo, because his name is associated so closely with Sanibel and its connecting sister island, Captiva. Stories about Gasparillo's career differ widely, depending on who is telling them. There is no documented evidence that he existed, in fact. But he is publicized as The Pirate of the region, with festivals, in the tourist season, celebrating his life; oversized effigies of him in the forecourts of motels; stories printed and widely circulated by real estate agents. He was supposed to have made his headquarters on Boca Grande, and to have accumulated 30 million dollars in cash, which he buried in pits on Little Gasparillo Key. He kept his captured females on Captiva, whence, supposedly, came its name. Sanibel was his hunting preserve, and from its southern beaches he conducted a profitable trade with the La Fitte brothers of New Orleans. Considering the poorness of his territory the loot seems large. Several facts argue against his existence: that the sloop and commander who are said to have captured him (one story claims that he avoided capture by wrapping the anchor chain around his neck and throwing himself into the sea) were at that time actually 250 miles away off Cape Antonio, Cuba, disposing of an undoubtedly real gang of pirates on the rich Europe–South America run; that no record of his name or that of any of his crew is noted in the records of the federal court or any other state papers; that Gasparillo Island was named on all English and Spanish maps long before his time, probably for a missionary in the time of Menéndez. Captiva also appears on earlier charts, as part of Sanibel. None of this actually disproves his existence, but it casts a strong doubt. In any case there is no need to glorify a pirate who, if he did live, was no more than a small-time thug.

Sanibel has been through the years a haven for other disreputable activities. Its inlets, hidden by dense mangrove, invite illegal entry. Bootlegged slaves were brought in; later, during Prohibition, rum from Havana; still later, in the '30's and '40's, European refugees without visas, who had to pay a large price for their freedom. The most recent import is drugs. Sometimes these cargos, human or freight, had to be dumped precipitately into the sea. In fact, from the arrival of the first greedy Spaniard to the latest drug-peddling gangster, human kindness has not been a factor in the exploitation of the islands.

After the Caloosas had been driven off, Sanibel was not regarded as a place to live for many years, but was inhabited only briefly by the riffraff who found it a sanctuary. The growth of the west coast of Florida as a tourist attraction was far slower than that of the east. The Atlantic coast had been discovered earlier as a suitable stretch of beautiful beach on which to build enormous hotels, and the railroad lines went there. The Gulf coast seemed too far away. However, in 1883, people came to live in Sanibel, not pirates or blockade-runners or those seeking illegal entry; not even tourists. Farmers came, and cleared the land and planted. Every square foot of arable land was given over to citrus trees, tomatoes, eggplants, squashes. Sanibel bloomed again, as it had in the days of the Caloosas. The soil, away from the marshes and the beaches, was and is remarkably fertile. One gardener received $1,100 for tomatoes grown on one acre in the year 1901. But it seemed that Sanibel did not want a population. Hurricanes swept over the island with depressing regularity, and in 1926 a particularly severe one destroyed all the crops and drove the farmers off.

Only a few people stayed, and they did not farm. They catered to a small group of winter and spring visitors who came to fish off the beach and search for rare shells. Many of those settlers are still there, and the same faithful visitors come back year after year, with children and grandchildren, deploring the changes but still coming, picking up shells on one of the great shell-collecting beaches in the western hemisphere, still surf casting, still looking with wonder at the masses of migrating shorebirds that darken the beaches in

March and the magnificent flight of roseate spoonbills in the evenings.

This old group of residents and annual visitors is not growing smaller but it is beginning to seem insignificant. In 1964 a bridge was built from Punta Rassa on the mainland across San Carlos Bay to Sanibel, replacing the car ferries. With the bridge, inevitably, came the land developers. After the farmers had left in 1926 the island rapidly grew wild again, and it was nearing climax. But bulldozers are ensuring that natural full growth will not come, except in a few protected pockets. Even these cannot be protected much longer, with new roads being built all along the beach. The only hope, and it is not a kind one, is that a hurricane will take charge again and wipe it all off: the motels, the coy gift shops and dress shops, the boxlike houses beside muddy man-made canals in squares denuded of trees. It would have to be an extraordinarily destructive hurricane, and much that is good would go too. But the trees, most of them, would stay, and the birds would come back as soon as the wind died down. Some of the people would return too, those who are used to hurricanes. But this is a forlorn thought. As long as the bridge is there, Sanibel is liable to be developed and engulfed. No legislation can help it. Money is in charge.

2.

*A*bout half the island is difficult to tamper with, though sooner or later some way will probably be found to drain it for housing projects. For the present it is inviolate, consisting of shallow salt lakes and inlets and dense clusters of mangroves growing straight out of black water. Bare grayed trunks extend about a foot above the water, almost invisible beneath the foliage, giving the groves the appearance of levitation. The tide causes this, but it is strange to see groups of trees apparently suspended in the air like mirages.

On the arched mangrove buttresses live small sweet oysters,
and in the branches pelicans roost at night.

Mangroves live on tropical coasts of America and the west coast of Africa. It is thought that the American mangroves crossed from Africa by way of the equatorial current, and they are probably still doing so. Fossil records go back to the Cenozoic period about 45 million years ago, near the time when Florida came up out of the sea. Though they belong to the highest group of plants, the seed bearers, whose earliest forms developed on land, they have gone back to the sea. Possibly competition with other plants forced them into salt water. Whatever the reason, they are now so successful in their difficult surroundings that no other plant can threaten them. They grow where nothing else can, but it is possible that they cannot grow where other plants are.

Less than half of a mangrove's seedlings remain near the parent tree. The rest float horizontally, all over the warm oceans, drifting for months, able to survive sun, rain and rough water. Eventually the future root end becomes heavy, weighted by a smooth case, and the new plant seeks a new home. Pointed now downward it drifts vertically. When it crosses shallow water it is likely to find a little ridge or shoal, and there the sharp point meets sand and immediately embeds itself, breaks its shell and spreads roots wide and deep in the earth. As soon as the root is firmly entrenched the tree begins to grow, and its young branches send shoots downward to arch in a protecting buttress.

Sanibel and much of the Gulf coast of Florida offered refuge to the rootless, leafless plants that had traveled who knows how many months or years from a far continent. The shallow quiet water of the bay side of the island, protected from the open-water south side by shell ridges formed by Gulf storms, gave them a good home. They dropped their re-markably clawlike tentacles through the water down into the sand and shell, which provided all the nourishment they needed, and proceeded to make a living place out of a bleak, bleached accident of the ocean which one severe hurricane would have washed underwater again. Leaves appeared, small and dark green, above the high tide line, and little yellow flowers that bloom almost all year round. As soon as each mangrove tree was strong enough to support offspring, new shoots developed on its branches and grew into heavy seedlings, six to eight inches long. Instead of heading upward, toward light, like most trees, many of the shoots descended, like the original parent tree, into the water. The dead leaves provided a mulch, along with the bodies of marine creatures, shrimps hiding from fish and herons among the tangle growth of stems, and small sweet oysters growing thickly along the branches just at the tide line. Soil was made, and after a while other plants could grow in it. Sanibel became green, its plant growth anchoring it against storm and tide, so it is no longer an unstable wash of shifting sand but a true island, with its own pace of growth and decay, independent as any island can be of its original creator, the sea.

Red mangroves, those advancing into salt water, give a deceptive impression of mild climate. Columbus thought that there could be no storms where trees rooted in the edge of the sea. But after a hurricane has passed, taking roofs off buildings, knocking over palm trees, making new beaches and destroying roads in the following tidal waves, the mangrove forest is still there, serene as ever, an indestructible jungle. Only severe frost can damage the leaves, and even then the denseness of the foliage protects all but the outer leaves. Cold weather usually leaves Florida alone, and a light frost does no harm to the island makers. They are superbly successful plants in their specialized habitat, awe-inspiring in their continuing march over bays and inlets. Sanibel is getting bigger all the time. While the south wind piles up new shells and sand on the outer beach the mangroves creep visibly across the shallow lagoons of the inner shore.

Only in the evening is this dreamlike setting visibly inhabited. Then come the spectacular marsh birds, to stand tall near the mangroves, reflected without a ripple in the red water of sunset.

Until the middle of this century hardly anyone knew of this jungle-protected haven. A canoe can pass with difficulty between the thick groves to reach the lakes where the birds spend their nights. Recently their existence was reported and steps were taken at once to protect them. The Fish and Wildlife Service, with the active assistance of the local Audubon Society, arranged to buy or lease about two thousand acres and set it aside as a sanctuary. Bottom soil, consisting almost entirely of shells, was dredged up to make a loop of road through one of the largest salt lakes, so people could see the great birds without being close enough to frighten or molest them. The sanctuary is named after J. N. "Ding" Darling, a well-known cartoonist and active conservationist. In the 1930's he persuaded Congress to buy many thousands of acres for the big vulnerable birds that are often shot for food or feathers, often unable to breed due to the draining of marshes — their feeding places — and the demolition of the tall trees in which they nest, and always helpless against our civilization.

Years ago it was rare to see a roseate spoonbill on the island. Once in a great while someone would report seeing one in a puddle back of the Gulf beach. No one conceived of Sanibel as one of the largest roseate spoonbill colonies ·on the Gulf coast. Now, however, many nest there; and many more go there after the young, born in rookeries in the southern Everglades and the Florida Keys in November, are fully fledged and turning pink. In the Sanibel mangroves they are more or less safe, protected by the impenetrable forest. Elsewhere they were pursued unmercifully. In 1879 they were the most abundant bird on the Gulf coast. Fifty years later they were almost extinct. Rose-colored, bright against the dark trees, they were easy targets for anyone with a gun — and nearly everyone along that coast has a gun. Farmers and fishermen killed them for food, first stripping off the glorious scarlet-patched wings for tourists to take north as fans. A young Fish and Wildlife Service employee who spent his summers on the coast in the 1950's trying to educate the hunters away from the "pink chickens," declared that they were as likely to shoot him as the birds. He and others succeeded, however. Though the roseate spoonbill will never again be abundant it will live on, provided the Everglades don't dry up completely.

In the Sanibel mangroves the big birds hide in the daytime, from heat and sun and possible hunters. But between five and six o'clock any evening from late January on through spring, the loop of road is almost as crowded and slow-moving as a city expressway during rush hour. Everyone is good-humored, no one wants to move fast. Cars pull off the road to watch an anhinga gyrating its neck, or a brown pelican feeding tamely a few yards out in the water, or bright warblers darting in and out of the trees that almost touch the road. The main objective, a bird-watching tower between the widest parts of the inland lakes, is approached slowly, as no one can advance the leisurely arrival of the spoonbills. They appear in the sky high and far away, at first one by one, then in increasingly large flocks. They come from all over the mangrove jungle, and circle in the sky, looking for their companions. The flight is slow, the landing graceful. They are all in by sunset, perhaps one or two hundred, and their colors are a reflection of the sky, varying from white to pale pink to carmine, with orange tails and bald greenish heads. As soon as each one lands it buries that bare head in the mud and moves the long broad-tipped bill sideways in a manner that looks ridiculous on such a flaming creature. To them it is not ridiculous. They are stirring up their food with their "spoons," to find any animals that live in the shallow mangrove water — insects, shrimps, snails, small fish. The flock is usually too far away to be shot at, and a telescope is needed to see them well. It seems that the spoonbills have learned their worst enemy, and know well how to keep out of his way. They have other enemies too, and they build their bulky nests of sticks in the middle of mangroves, about twelve feet above water, for safety from snakes and alligators. One priceless commodity is fast disappearing, and that is ground water. This is not on account of drought, but human greed. If we try hard enough we can dry up all Florida's swamps and make the peninsula into a tenantless desert. By good fortune there is no industry on Sanibel, and it is not one of the big popular tourist areas. What animals and vegetation are still there will probably remain.

One of the threatened species is not a Sanibel nester, but builds its large nests in the crowns of trees in the Everglades and Corkscrew Swamp. That is the wood ibis, our only stork. They were never in memory plentiful, but we used to see groups of a dozen or so gliding on enormous white, black-edged wings. The big birds, weighing up to ten pounds, flew without a motion of wing, except an effortless angling to take advantage of air currents over Sanibel's salt and brackish ponds. Their long legs streamed behind the short black tails, and when they came in to land the legs came up under them to touch the water first. Not a ripple stirred as they brought their six-foot wings forward, folded them down and landed in a standing posture, feet down, dark heads in the water, all in one motion. The birds moved slowly, singly or in pairs, hunting for minnows and other small animals. Never did a head come up. Every few seconds one of the thin claws came forward to stir up the mud, so close to the beak that it seemed to be scratching. They were liberating their prey. A wood ibis in captivity will eat three dozen shrimp at a time. In the wild state its intake is much larger, and while nesting it will fly sixty or more miles a day in search of food to feed not only itself but its nestling, which is larger than the parent at the time of leaving the nest. As its food lives entirely in swampy areas or shallow lakes, in times of drought the wood ibis can barely subsist and will not breed. When the rain has been unusually heavy it also has a hard time, as it cannot reach the mud below. There are about four thousand ibis in Florida. Because of the draining and development of the area north of the Everglades they have been largely forced to move elsewhere, and for several years those that remained did not breed at all. Frost also hurts them, destroying their eggs. They may be one of the vanishing species, and we feel lucky to see a few birds in Sanibel's mangrove sanctuary. They hunch, long necks arched, looking like nothing so much as immense croquet wickets. The delicate rustling of wing and tail, feathering in the wind, does not seem to go with this large, clumsy bird. Beside them the spoonbills are dainty. There is a great difference between a length of twenty-eight inches, which is the spoonbill, and the much stouter three feet of wood ibis. If they are seen together in flight, the difference is even more marked — the ibis has a foot more of wingspread.

The sanctuary is not only the evening feeding place of these great birds. Black skimmers, sleek and long-winged, range low over the water, their beaks slightly open so that the knife-edged lower mandible, longer than the upper, can easily scoop up the small fish that come near the surface late in the day. Even after the sun has set the skimmers scour the water in wide, circular flights, their slim bodies never touching the surface, only the heavy red and black beaks leaving slight ripples behind them. Large numbers of herons and white ibis inhabit this rich area. The white ibis are beautiful fliers, delicate and slim, black wing tips sharp against the sky. Before they go to roost in the branches of the trees at sunset they circle in dazzling flocks, alighting now and again to feed. Like the spoonbills they enjoy one another's company. The herons are solitary. The little blue, the great blue, the Louisiana, the snowy egret, the American egret stand each in his own place watching the water, absolutely still, long beak pointed forward and downward. Swifter than a snake the head descends, and a small fish goes visibly down the gullet. When not eating they perch for hours at a time on an exposed branch. At the end of the loop of road there is a post, weathered and slate-gray. It is an ordinary post, except for its top. We looked for a few minutes to see why the top was distorted. Even through binoculars the little blue heron hunched there looked like a carving, part of the post that a fanciful workman had shaped one easy day. The bird was the same color as its perch and it did not so much as blink an eye.

There are a few brown pelicans in the water of the sanctuary. Generally they prefer open, deeper water for feeding, but they come in to the mangroves to roost. Ten thousand pelicans roost and nest in and around the sanctuary, and in the evening they come to their night homes, which have a powdered look from their droppings. Ten thousand of almost any other bird — fulmars on a northern cliff, petrels in underground burrows — can be reasonably encompassed by mind or eye. But a bird forty-one inches long, with a six-and-a-half-foot wingspread, tightly colonizing the low mangroves, is a sight to be reckoned with, an incredible congregation. They are a solid weight, brown and white and mottled, pressing the branches even lower. But the next morning, when the pelicans have gone, the trees have sprung up again. Sometimes they feed in the shallow water before retiring near dark. We watched one near the road. It moved quietly through the water, not seeming to use any part of its body in locomotion. Suddenly it hopped, wings half outspread, dipped its heavy ten-inch bill into the water and raised it immediately. The fish wriggled in its loose pouch; then, after some gargling while the water was drained out, the bird pointed its bill skyward and the fish slid down its gullet. Pelicans are easy marks for gulls, which will light on the big bird's head and lean into the beak to snatch a fish out of the gullet.

Many ducks winter in the inland lakes, some bright-plumaged, some drab. They swim slowly and placidly, sometimes upending in the shallow water, where even diving ducks have to behave like puddle ducks. The only active ones are young red-breasted mergansers, and their conduct is astonishing. You see them in the distance, a long straight line disturbing the water, and at first they appear to be a school of fish breaking water to escape a larger fish. As you come near you see what is happening, but not why. They splash, skitter over the water, turn and whirl, always keeping in their line. We stayed for an hour the first time, and they still did this. The next day it was the same, and the next. They were not fishing, because for that they dive. They have been known to swim on an extended front, in a line, driving their prey before them to the very shallow water where they can pick up the fish easily with their serrated bills. But this line wasn't driving anything. It stayed in the same place, single file, head to tail, and the birds were apparently playing. Once in a while one left the line and ran through the water very fast, without using its wings. Since the feet were invisible it seemed to glide. Then it slid back into formation and resumed splashing and gyrating.

Farther along the sanctuary loop the trees close in and there is only a canal between the people and the trees, dug by the machines that dredged mud out of the swamp and made it into a road. There one is in closer contact with the birds, those which are not afraid. We stood at the edge of the road staring at a red-shouldered hawk cunningly hidden on a red-brown branch. He fitted there, invisible, like a piece of jigsaw puzzle, and at first we saw only eyes, staring back at us. For a few minutes we faced each other, all unmoving; then the hawk silently flew off his branch. He astonished a little blue heron that had been standing equally still and imperceptible. The heron squawked indignantly and flapped up from the shore, its beak open, actually touching the hawk. Each was thoroughly startled by the other's presence, and both disappeared back into the forest.

The next contact was an anhinga, known locally as snake-bird. She clung to a low branch with enormous yellowish webbed feet, holding her wings out to dry. The anhinga noticed us as we got out of the car, but was not ready to depart. Wings still spread, she slithered her neck around, pointed her sharp beak at us from several directions, and grunted. Her snake-dance ritual held us. It was graceful and grotesque at the same time, and the anhinga appeared more reptile than bird. The neck was long and thin, and the small head and long beak seemed a continuation. The short feathers of the neck were ruffled from water and resembled pale brown fur. However strange it looks, the anhinga is a highly capable bird. In the water it dips below the surface and prowls slowly. When a victim (fish, water snake, small alligator, even turtle) is secured by the pointed beak — skewered actually — the bird comes up to flip its catch and swallow it. If the victim has too many edges, or is too big, the bird will pound it against the nearest hard object.

In flight the anhinga is glorious. It rises, alternately flapping and circling on its broad wings until it is a small cross against the sky. Then it will suddenly fold its wings and drop straight down. In the water it has a further specialty. If it feels threatened it cuts down on its internal air and sinks slowly, swimming backward with those great membraned feet, until only part of its neck and narrow head are above the surface. For such a primitive creature, only a few steps removed from its progenitors, the flying reptiles of the Jurassic age of about 150 million years ago, it gets along excellently in the modern world.

The one that was grunting angrily at us probably had a large sloppy nest nearby, as she and her mate (whose neck feathers are darker and silver-spotted) are silent unless they think their young are threatened. The nest was safe from us and anyone else, well hidden in the dark leaves, but the young are naked when they come out of the eggs, and terribly vulnerable to any climbing animal such as a raccoon or a bobcat, or to a hungry hawk. The numbers of anhingas on Sanibel are vast compared to those of their predators, and their threatening appearance is a strong deterrent. It is not a species to worry about. Though its chief residence in the United States is the marshland and lake districts of southern Florida it can also live near secluded bays, having adapted itself to salt as well as brackish and fresh water. So it can survive drought and draining, and as long as the Gulf waters are relatively uncontaminated, it is safe.

These are only a few of the 240 species of birds that make their home on Sanibel Island. The heavy foliage is a home or a migration stopover for many kinds of warblers. Deep among the arched roots rails feed contentedly. Gulls and terns find a resting place from their ceaseless hunting over the open Gulf. Flocks of sandpipers and plovers, mostly in migration time,

The sanctuary's shallow reed-bound lake is a haven for ducks and herons as well as the spectacular storks and spoonbills.

swing and dip in unison over the shallow water, coming to rest finally on the narrow beach below the road. The black skimmers try to go to sleep on the road itself, flying reluctantly out of the way when a car comes, back again as soon as it has gone. Undoubtedly the road, so busy with people in the daytime, is a haven at night for birds that roost on the ground and like to keep their feet dry. The sanctuary belongs to its multitude of birds and not, happily, to the humans, who go only to watch and wonder.

3.

*A*fter the five-mile circuit of the mangrove lakes, finished
with reluctance as the sun sets, we reach a side road that leads
to the main highway. There is a little trail off this side road,
but it should be approached on a cool windy day, when there
are slightly fewer mosquitoes. It is not a large area. In a short
walk you can see one of the sanctuary lakes with its mangrove
border. But within its confines it is another world. History is
around you — history centuries old and history no more than
forty years ago, all hidden by the heavy quick-growing semi-

tropical growth that covers even the most recent developments.

A few minutes after entering the small overgrown trail a sweet-tart scent came to us. It emanated from a grove of citrus trees surrounded by laurels. The trees were limes, planted in the 1920's by one of Sanibel's farmers who was driven out, or preferred not to stay, after the hurricane of 1926. Both blossoms and fruit were there together. The flowers were miniature orange blooms and smelled the same, though fainter. The limes were yellowish, with thin skins and a great deal of juice. We picked up the falls and used them in drinks. They were far tastier than usual fruit-store limes, for no known reason.

The lime plantation was on a small round hill that consisted, it seemed entirely, of oyster and whelk shells. Perhaps the shell fragments had a beneficial influence on the soil, to produce such volume and perfection of fruit after forty years of neglect. The laurels, too, were thick-leaved healthy plants, undoubtedly set in by the colonist as a beautiful and protective hedge around his limes. Among the plants and trees planted by men is a large native tree, the gumbo-limbo, a big twisted tree with smooth reddish naked branches and thick small green leaves that are incongruous on the fat limbs. The tree looks tortured, no branch being straight; but wind does not touch it. It just grows that way, standing out spectacularly among the small lime trees.

Looking for fallen limes we came across broken bits of red and black pottery and realized that we were in an ancient Caloosa area. Their main item of diet was the abundant shellfish, and of that by far the most numerous were whelks and mangrove oysters, the flat little oysters that grow in profusion along the lower parts of the mangrove trees, just above low tide line, studding the reddish trunks and buttresses like uneven scales. Near here the Sanibel Caloosa colony had its dwellings, probably right on this site. This is easily deduced by the height of the hill. Sanibel is nowhere above fourteen feet, and hurricane tides wash over it frequently. But the Indians built high, on accumulated shells, and the lime grove was high in comparison with the near sea level of the Florida peninsula and its islands. The bay was close, only a few yards beyond the thicket of undergrowth and the screen of mangroves, all new growth. The Indians' shell-lined canals would have led easily into Pine Island Sound. The intricacy and sophistication of the settlement is long gone, deliberately destroyed by the Spanish. Now, between the lime trees, grow poison ivy and cactus, almost impenetrable, and mosquitoes breed there in millions. Day and night, all year round, they ply their trade. How did the Caloosas get along with them? Possibly, knowing the local plants so intimately, they had discovered a juice that repelled mosquitoes. Or else they just lived with them, as many local residents do now, without complaint. A fishing guide, born and bred on the mainland across from Sanibel, said it was best to be there in summer. "What about mosquitoes?" I said. "Well, I guess there'll be a few mosquitoes around — but you should see the tarpon!"

The area is richer generally in summer than in winter. Starting in April is the wonderful flowering season, when the air is rich with color and scent. In the lime grove prickly pear and the Spanish bayonet flower. Night-blooming cereus is everywhere, its limp green strands, unable to support their own weight, leaning against the gumbo-limbo trees. Only in the heat and dampness of full summer would the twelve-inch white blossoms open at night and release their legendary fragrance until daybreak.

Papaya, an herb that looks like a tree, is a tropical plant, cultivated in southern Florida and gone wild. It is at its best at the height of summer, when its large clusters of yellow

193

flowers open, to give way to the melonlike fruit. Even in spring some papayas bear fruit, though it is a barren-looking plant. The eye travels up and up the bare unbranched trunk, expecting nothing, then at the top, perhaps twenty feet, encounters a surprising crown of enormous, deeply indented leaves, with pendulous green or yellow fruits just below them.

Coconuts grow their blossoms, which look not so much like flowers as long golden hair. The pineapple air plant, living high on dead trees where it can get a maximum of sun and rain, sprouts long thin stems that droop over in a crimson flowering. Wherever there was a patch of sunlight the dark spotted leaves of the succulent called life plant spread thickly, with a host of trumpet-shaped blossoms hanging downwards from a straight tall stem, and the curled leaves carry on their edges complete new plants with their own roots and flowers. Most beautiful of all and now, unfortunately, hardly more to be seen, are butterfly orchids, a spray of delicate yellow that would sell for a minor fortune in a florist's shop. They have been taken by the few who always want to pick everything. There used to be many in the lime grove; now there are none.

We have seen all these flowers except the night-blooming cereus — the gangly cactus that doesn't look as if it could produce anything but thorns. But we have not seen them in their glory, when everything is full out at once. Much as we missed in summer, we were glad to be there only in early spring, on a cool day with the wind coming off Pine Island Sound. The combination of cactus, succulent, laurel, lime and air plant, all in one small area, showed the abundance of Sanibel's plant life. Desert, mountain and tropic were represented in profusion, and showed that anything could grow in this favorable, mild climate. Sanibel has three hundred species of native plants. Sometimes it is dry, and the cacti thrive. Night-blooming cereus, a desert cactus, is luxuriant in this place so far from any desert. Often it is cold, and the mountain laurel can grow tall and thick. In damp parts of the earth small succulents found their needs fulfilled.

The lime grove is particularly thick with the air plants associated with our southeast. Pineapple air plants are surrounded by circles of infants. Their pointed leaves widen at the base to an ample tank, which holds water enough to support, not only themselves but mosquito larvae and families of snails and small frogs. In dry weather they do not die but merely cease to produce flowers. One good shower restores them. The most familiar of the air plant genus (*Tillandsia*) is Spanish moss, not a moss at all. In the warm season it produces small inconspicuous yellow flowers and thin hairy fruits. It has no roots, but clings to branches and hangs to the ground in long tangled gray strings. The slender stems and leaves are covered with fine hairs, and collect dust. In the dust is its food and water. It is a truly economical and well-regulated plant. If we could live on dust alone how little would we waste the liberality of nature.

4.

A goodly amount of Sanibel is given over to sanctuary. An older refuge on the island is the Bailey Sanctuary, a hundred-acre tract on Tarpon Bay Road, not far from the Gulf beach. Before Florida's years of drought, Bailey Sanctuary had lakes and man-made canals surrounded by reeds and a small group of mangroves in the middle which, near evening, was the favored rookery of white ibis, wood ibis, pelicans and herons. One would stand on the observation tower with the strong smell of sulphur springs rising from below, and watch them all come in large flocks just as the sun was setting. In the shallow lakes, as early as the first week in March, a pair of stilts had come to breed, slim and unbelievably elegant, deep black and sharp white patterned, with very long red legs. Blue-winged teal, gallinules and coots were there in quantity. With the dropping of the water table all these birds have gone over to the new sanctuary, which is continuously supplied by the tides. On the muddy edges rails, fat as chickens, with little upturned tails, fed in the reeds. Rails, contrary to general thought, are not shy. They are just difficult to see in the shadows. Sometimes we glimpsed them from the top of the tower, other times while walking along the raised trails and looking down the canals. We watched them move placidly within a few yards of us, their extra long thick claws supporting them on the mud.

Bailey Sanctuary was the place to go for marsh birds. With the opening of the "Ding" Darling Sanctuary, however, the old one has been neglected. Where the lakes were, reeds have almost entirely taken over. The water is not visible from any of the overgrown trails. Part of the reason was the dropping of the water table during the drought years. There actually is not much water left. Here and there you can see through to the wet earth, and you know that whatever man has done or failed to do, many birds are still there. Rails are abundant. Swamp sparrows scratch over and over on the same piece of ground, and nothing will scare them away. The swampy ground supports a wilderness of coarse grasses, of leather ferns — tall, bronze-green, heavy leaved — of cattails, as high as six feet, a marsh plant too attractive for its own good, exterminated in many parts of the east by overpicking. At times there are hundreds of robins in the little trees, and myrtle and black-and-white warblers are constant all winter. The commonest resident is the red-winged blackbird. The mangroves

A pair of black-necked stilts comes back every year to nest near one of the hidden ponds of the Bailey tract.

still have their evening visitors. You hear the continuous hollow notes of coots and gallinules and the hoarse croaks of herons, though they are not to be seen in the little water that still hides below the undergrowth. Besides birds there are a few frogs and snakes, but March is a little early. In late spring and summer they will be plentiful. Large brown marsh rabbits are so unafraid that they will crouch in the middle of the trail until you almost step on them.

Along Tarpon Bay Road, which passes through the middle of Bailey Sanctuary, it used to be common to see alligators sunning themselves in the morning beside the water-filled ditches. Sometimes one would see them swimming in the then open water, only their square snouts showing. They are carnivorous but not dangerous to man; in fact they avoid him. A common alligator tactic is to catch the feet of a swimming duck, hold it under water until it drowns, then bring it up and eat it. The big ones, up to fifteen feet, can swallow a duck whole. There are not many in southern Florida now, as they have been killed wholesale for their attractive hides, and many of those that have been spared have died because of the drought. There may be a few still left in inland lakes on Sanibel, but the old sanctuary has none.

In spite of the loss of alligators Bailey Sanctuary, deserted, is a beautiful and wild and rich piece of land. Someday, perhaps its water will be restored by natural means — the bubbling up of the sulphur springs and the brackish water of the lakes and canals. For the animals that live there it is still a good place, probably better without the people who used to throng its trails and tower. Now I can close my eyes and hear the multitude of swamp sounds — croaks, whistles, twitters, never stopping.

5.

The still, life-teeming waters of the mangrove sanctuaries and the protected profusion of plant life in the lime grove are far removed from the Gulf side of Sanibel. Though only a mile or so to the south, the windy beach seems another part of the world entirely. A small back road leads to the beach, through typical mid-island scenery: squat saw palmettos and swamps with black and turkey vultures hovering over them; pileated woodpeckers digging noisily into posts; rough-grassed fields which used to be tomato plantations and are now, where not developed, haunts of meadowlarks and mockingbirds and, in the past few years, multitudes of the African cattle egret that found its way here across the Atlantic and has multiplied exceedingly (in spite of the absence of cattle). Then the road ends and one comes suddenly to a scene that makes the heart stop. The edge of the water is always exciting, whether at the bottom of steep cliffs, or gleaming through forest, or on the wide golden beaches of the mid-Atlantic coast. But there is nothing on the Atlantic, from Maine to Florida, that can compare with Sanibel's Gulf beach. The water is deeper blue than the sky, its small waves flecked with white. A salt mist is in the air, blown capriciously by light winds. At the edge of the water a snowy egret stands still, its plumes tossed, seeming to have the lightness of the wind mist. Beyond it, near shore, a family of dolphins plays fearlessly, turning over and over, arching and blowing, almost on the beach. The egret moves a little, lifting one slim bright yellow foot after the other, not to avoid the dolphins but to search for any small fish they might have frightened inshore. It is not a wide beach, and Australian pines hang over it, sighing and giving with the wind, and coconut palms grow just above high tide line, their long fronds whispering. Among these tall trees are thickets of sea grape: low-growing, twisted trees up to a hundred years old. Their large round red-veined leaves are so sturdy and leathery that the Spanish are said to have used them for stationery. Clumps of sea oats grow out of the squat dunes, keeping the upper beach in place when hurricane tides wash over it. Their dark gold heads, thick with grain, nod in the wind like the feathers of the egret. There are no doubt beaches lovelier in the world, but this is the one we know, and its beauty strikes us anew every time we see it.

It is a good beach to walk on, for it is heavily populated with shells of mollusks long dead, as well as new live creatures brought up with every tide. One day the water will bring in a host of serpent stars, their long thin rays twisting around the fingers when you pick them up. But they secrete a venomous liquid, and are capable of digesting live flesh. Another morning there will be hundreds of fat heavy starfish, many a foot or more in diameter, with nine arms instead of the usual five. They are so terrible to look at that, poisonous or not, we avoid them completely. Then there will be a day of the beautiful, deadly blue-green jellyfish, Portuguese man-of-war. I once came home with several of these cupped in both hands, enticed by the brilliant color to pick them up. I was met by a horrified old-timer who enjoined me to drop them instantly, saying I could be mortally poisoned. This is not precisely true. Like many other jellyfish the Portuguese men-of-war have stinging cells in their tentacles, for self-defense and for killing prey. On contact with humans these cells leave angry rashes. Those I held were apparently neither frightened nor hungry, because I was unmarked. However it was my first and last intimate encounter with these bright creatures.

Another high tide will leave a host of little round sea hearts (or "heart urchins"), whitened in death, with the sign of five, like all that family (echinoids), engraved so deeply that they resemble nothing so much as shrunken heads — shrunken down to about an inch. A few times the water brought up a different sort of life. The long seedlings of red mangroves, that float all over the world of warm water, occasionally found their way around from Pine Island Sound and gathered at the top of the beach. There they immediately put down roots and grew leaves, becoming a colony that only a storm could scatter. Little as they were, some being no more than two or three inches high, with only two leaves, the roots gripped deeply into the sand, resisting the plucking of the tides, and almost impossible to get up by hand.

The sand of Sanibel's Gulf beach is made of sun-bleached shells. A snowy egret hunts for small fish frightened inshore by dolphins.

The best-known attraction of Sanibel's eleven-mile beach is its shells. The sand we walk on is not ordinary sand made of rocks brought down by rivers and reduced to sand by wave action. It is composed entirely of shells, so finely ground that they cling to the feet like white dust. Overlying the shell-sand, and changing continuously, are innumerable whole shells as pleasing to the eye as classical statues, however ugly and warlike their once inhabitants were.

Mollusks are old in the history of the earth, and next to insects include more species than any other animal subdivision. Eighty thousand are known. It is thought that in the beginning, in the still mysterious Precambrian age over 600 million years ago when the earth's crust was forming, there were softbodied marine animals. But no fossils remain. Those early seas were acid, not yet containing the salts that seeped in later by erosion from the continents, and the new animals could not form shells. During the Cambrian age which followed, between 500 and 600 million years ago, the oceans accumulated calcium, and the small animals developed protective shells. Many can be found in fossil, and some exist still in almost their original form. Sanibel's Gulf coast, facing south, unlike the shores of its sister islands, favors a unique concentration of shellfish. By reason of its shallow water and temperate climate, and its open exposure to the northward-flowing Gulf Stream (which does flow north along Florida's west coast, though it reaches its strongest force in the narrow Florida Straits, where it meets the Atlantic), countless mollusks can grow there The island is built on shells. It owes its origin to the lifting of the land which took place over a long period during the Pleistocene era, the geologic age just before our own. Sanibel is a new island in geologic history, going back no more than ten million years, when the whole Florida peninsula slanted up out of the water. During the latest ice age the ocean level fell, and southern Florida and its islands appeared. Before that the water stood about one hundred feet higher than it does now, and there were no islands. In fact there was no southwest Florida, and land began 150 miles north of the Keys.

Below the water then was ooze composed of many sea animals and a solution of limestone. This solidified into white limestone and forms the base rock under the peninsula and its surrounding ocean. Beneath Sanibel's shell crust is this fine white rock, not visible at any place on the island. We never found a pebble. The only approximation of rock that we picked up was a piece of marl, a sand-colored cementlike bit of sea bottom covered on both sides with the shells of mollusks, and honeycombed with their borings. Marl forms a main part of the sediments that go to make up Sanibel's soil. Its partners are sand and silt. The soil has little organic matter and loses water rapidly. But the annual rainfall of between fifty and sixty inches, and the long growing season, compensate. The island is extraordinarily fertile, supporting plants of the temperate, tropical and subtropical zones.

The beach itself is still growing outward into the Gulf, the constant assault of water from the south bringing, not erosion but fine-ground shells. You can see the change from year to year. The beach becomes no wider but it changes. Where last year there was only fine sand at the top of the beach, this year there will be no beach there, but a new shell ridge with sea oats and shrubs well established, and here and there a buried coconut sending up wide young fronds.

You start for a stroll on the firm sand of the water's edge. You really want only to walk, but there is a group of willets to attract the attention, waiting almost until you are upon them before they suddenly whir into the air, wings brilliantly white-patterned. Beyond them a ring-billed gull drops a clam repeatedly from on high, to break its shell. A little flock of sanderlings follow the receding tide, picking many-colored coquinas out of the wet sand before they can upend and dig themselves far down. You intend firmly not to be distracted again from walking, but you look up to the line where sand meets greenery and find the young mangroves establishing themselves. Of course you have to go up and try to get one out, and you admire their perseverance as you cut your fingers on shells that the long roots have entangled. Right behind the mangroves is a large deposit of sea hearts, an animal hardly ever seen alive. They spend their lives buried in mud or sand beneath shallow water, and move slowly by means of the spines that cover their bodies. From their excavated little rooms some six inches or more below wet sand they keep channels open with sticky mucus, and through these they can reach to the floor of the sea for the diatoms and other particles of food among the sand grains. The deep furrows on their egg-shaped bodies enable them to sustain a current of water through which the sediment has been strained. By this means they breathe and excrete, until some upheaval, probably an extra high tide combined with a strong wind — like an earthquake to them — tosses them to the surface, where they lose their spines and drift lightly, for they are very thin-cased, up to the top of the high tide line. Highly specialized as they are, needing a certain kind of environment and no other (and flourishing exceedingly there), it is sad to see them flung from their element in whitened heaps amid the dead seaweed and driftwood.

Scattered through the jetsam behind the mangroves are the half-inch cones of Australian pines, and you stop to admire the red-barked trees, graceful and strong. They were planted here about sixty years ago to bind the soil and break the wind.

Australian they are, pines they are not. Their genus name is Casuarina, and they are native to the South Pacific though widely introduced in the western hemisphere as shade trees. A downward-hanging branch reveals that the "needles" are straight twigs with small leaves clinging as close as scales. They are evergreen, but can only grow where there is little frost. The wood, extremely hard and valued for building, is known as beefwood for its dark red color. Among the Australian pines are coconut palms growing contentedly in dry sand. They are far wanderers, and no one knows their original point of departure. The exceptionally large fruit, which is actually one enormous seed, floats easily and almost indefinitely on account of the lightness of its fibrous husk and the water-inpenetrable leathery skin. Eventually the nut comes to land and buries itself in sand, liking salt water and salt earth. It will grow perhaps forty years, and attain a height of one hundred feet, with a crop of as many as four hundred and fifty nuts each year, clustered at the top, among the long fronds. It has no bark and no branches, and in fact bears only a superficial resemblance to a tree. Its nearest relatives are grasses, sedges and bananas. The dead fronds do not fall, but plait themselves together to form a trunk, its upper part hanging loose like sheets of coarse gray linen. Though not as elegant as many palms the coconut palm is almost excessively picturesque, leaning low over the sand, its head like an outsized feather nodding and murmuring in the wind.

As we walk back to the edge of the sea again, a diagonal single file of pelicans catches our eye as they glide along the water, nearly touching its surface. They hardly move their wings. Then one breaks from the line and rises with slow strong wing beats, the slowest of any bird's, taking about one and a half seconds for a complete cycle. A long way up, possibly sixty feet, the pelican stops abruptly and plunges straight into the water, to land with a large crash. It dives with open wings, but the instant the bird touches water it closes them, at the same time twisting so it will come up facing into the wind, ready for takeoff. This is a nice calculation for any bird, let alone one as seemingly ungainly as a pelican. During the dive it gulps the fish it has spotted from above, along with about three and a half gallons of sea water, then in the next second it is riding the slight swell in placid comfort. Takeoff is not so easy, even upwind, and a lot of action goes into it. They are heavy birds, and clumsily they fight air and water until once more they are up, and gliding with their huge wings barely off the waves. Though they roost inland they prefer open sea, where they can sail and dive at leisure, to the mangrove lakes, which do not offer them room for maneuver. They eat nothing but fish, and have been accused in the past of being harmful to human interests. In fact the white pelicans, their much larger relatives, were almost extinguished on account of this prejudice. Now it is known that less than one percent of the fish they eat is edible to man. In the Gulf they live on "trash fish," the oily menhaden that is common here and totally uninteresting to human fish eaters.

All they do — gliding, soaring, diving, floating, eating — is accomplished in silence. Most of the other seabirds we watched called and cried continuously. But the silent pelicans are not always thus: when they are still in the nest they bark and grunt incessantly. We have never seen a nest. The young hatch around Christmas, and sometime we must venture to skip this home holiday if only to hear the racketing of the nestlings — whether for want of food, or pleasure at being alive, or fighting one another, cannot be guessed.

Even while watching the pelicans we still walked. But at our feet a whelk suddenly jumped, then another and another.

Fiercely they writhed and leaped, trying to get back into the receding tide that had left them there. We threw some back in, but knew they would die anyway within an hour or two. Violent though they seemed, the lethal air had already stopped their vital processes. While trying to save them we saw a prettier sight, and a happier one. The little many-colored clams called coquinas also lay outside the tide line, but they would live a longer time, encased tightly within their mantles. When we tried to pick them up they did what frustrated many a shorebird. They upended on their points and disappeared immediately beneath the wet sand, where they could live until the tide came back again. They inhabit the tide line, tumbled up on the beach by waves, burrowing in with a small muscular foot when deserted, then again tossed out by a new wave.

Coquinas and whelks belong among two of the five main divisions of mollusks, the others being cephalopods (which include octopuses), chitons, and tusk shells. The coquina is an innocuous bivalve, but the whelk is a snail and a menace. Those that were struggling on the beach were fighting conchs, and they eat mostly clams. Along with most of their order they can penetrate the living shell with a proboscis called a radula, which has sharp teeth along it and acts as a saw. The snail sucks the living flesh out of the clam without even opening its shells. Most of the bivalves empty along the beach had a single small hole near the hinges, through which a snail had dined.

The coquina and its relatives feed more gently, subsisting on the plankton of the upper part of the water, or minute vegetable or animal matter from the mud, depending on their habitat. The tiny food organisms are drawn through a siphon and passed over the gills.

The most conspicuous shell on the beach, a bivalve, is the

pen shell, and it has been estimated that about a million have been thrown up on the beach in a single storm. It grows up to nine inches long, dark gray-brown, with a prickly surface. When in the water it anchors itself to the bottom by means of threads. In the old days, in the Mediterranean, these threads were spun into cloth of gold, delicate as a spider's web. Unprepossessing though they are the pens contain a lot of life if they are found just after being washed up. Lady's ear shells live in there amid seaweed adorned by an occasional thin simnia and worm shell and the little bright oysters called jewel boxes. Pen shells are havens for many small creatures that find life hard on their own because they are naturally little or are in the process of growing.

Once in a while there was a half angel wing, another bivalve, one of the most powerful of the boring clams. It is a beautiful pure white shell, its back covered with ridges that look like calcified feathers. As a live animal, however, it is unattractive, its big gray-pink body obscuring the shell. It has a very long siphon, necessary because its life is lived deep in mud and it has to maintain contact with the water. Buried as it is, it is safe from enemies. But divers have found that this well-insulated, hidden animal, glows with green light.

Skate egg cases, pillow-shaped black purses with thorny points on the four corners, sometimes contain live baby skates. At our hotel a dedicated student of the smaller animals of the sea slit one egg case open with a sharp knife and released the skate, a small pink version of its parents. It lived in her aquarium, still attached by a thread from its navel to its case, but it died early.

Other egg cases that wash up on the beach are those of whelks, curving strings of translucent tissue plates narrowing almost to nothing at the end, as if the parent had run out of eggs. Inside each of these cases a small whelk can be seen, an identical miniature of the adult. Tulip shell cases are a cluster of thin podlike containers on a stem, the whole looking like a flower, dead but still erect. Tulips themselves are rounded snails with pointed ends, reddish or banded, almost irresistible to pick up, shaped smooth as they are, their gentle whorls a reflection of the sea that made them so. Sometimes, in shallow water at low tide, one sees them apparently walking around, moving fairly fast. What is moving is actually a hermit crab which has chosen this roomy cell to live in, protecting its soft abdomen. These crabs are ferocious, attacking their own kind, but they quickly retreat to shelter before creatures that eat crabs.

The boat shell is a snail with a modified shell, having a half deck on the under surface. One often finds them attached together, one on top of the other, half a dozen or more. Each boat snail is male in the beginning, becoming female later. Those at the bottom of the chain are always females, a type of arrangement almost human. They are streaked brown, not always smooth. The odd one has small blunt prickles on it. They are vegetarians, feeding on diatoms which flow in through the mantle and are sieved through the gills.

One shell, usually found old and whitened by the sun, is the horse conch. It has a Victorian look, large (up to two feet) and rough, with knobbed ridges, the kind of semi-Bohemian decoration that one used to find on mantelpieces or in curio cabinets. It has a large opening, and you can listen to the sea in it. Its top end is pointed, its bottom end blunted and slightly open. In the old days, when we first knew Sanibel, a horse conch was blown into to summon us to dinner. The sound is hollow and muted, but carries enough to be heard down on the beach and in all the cottages. It is an eerie and beautiful way to be called. Sometimes we didn't know what it was. The sound is similar to the call of the ocean inside the shell. In its youth the horse conch is small and bright orange with a white tip, a pretty little snail. When alive the animal is among the most aggressive snails and eats bivalves and other snails, sucking them out of their shells. We have seen similar very large ones farther south, where collectors hang them up in the sun until the animal falls out. They are collected there for the mother-of-pearl interior, which gives them an added value in sale. We brought home a Sanibel horse conch shell, whitened and almost porous, and set a pineapple air plant in it. The arrangement looked attractively old-fashioned.

Lightning whelks are common on the beach. The name describes them: curved thin lines all the way down from the shallow tip to the narrow end. Their color is usually light brown, vivid when they are alive. They feed almost entirely on hard-shelled clams, which they envelop in their strong, large foot and force the clam's valves to open. They are dangerous-looking animals, slim and strong.

The junonia is an elegant creature, long and spotted and cream-colored, rarely found, and valued for its beauty. It is large (four inches in maturity) and carnivorous, but its food is only the small invertebrate marine animals with which the ocean teems.

An enticingly smooth shiny snail is the olive, which is sometimes found in great numbers on the beach, other times not at all. It is mottled brown, with a sharp whorled tip. Very rarely is found a color variation, an albino, actually golden yellow. Even rarer is another albino olive, gleaming white. When found alive the foot and mantle of the animal almost entirely cover the shell. That is what makes it glimmer as with polish. Olives are carnivorous, like most snails, and burrow into the sand for their small food.

The scallop family is enormous. Most usual on the Sanibel beach are calico scallops, whitish, mottled with red or brown.

*Coconut palms bend before a gale, and shells wash high up
on the beach. At low tide rare mollusks will be stranded
at the water's edge.*

Less ordinary are lemon yellow or bright orange, with no flecks. Once in a while one finds a fan, one valve of which is flat as if it had been ironed, the other valve deeply curved. The rarest there is the lion's paw, a strong-ribbed scallop with knobs along the ridges. All these scallops are irresistible, and we always come back with baskets of them, the commoner species to be reluctantly left for the next comer. Though they and all bivalves are the least intelligent of the mollusks, live scallops have eyes all along the mantle to the hinge, visible when they open their valves slightly. It is remarkable to look at those one hundred eyes that seem to be looking right back at you, with cornea, focusing lens, and retina. They resemble shining little jewels. Actually all they can see is motion and light. Scallops swim very well for a mollusk, facing frontwards with the valves horizontal, opening and shutting like mouths. When something alarms them they reverse and, snapping their valves, propel themselves backwards violently, bubbles shooting out behind them. Sometimes a diver may see great schools of scallops migrating somewhere, probably to find a different temperature of water. They eat microscopic free-floating plants, pumping water through the slightly open shells to filter out the food.

A pretty little snail, not often found, is the top shell, a shallow, flat-bottomed cone topped with a layer of mother-of-pearl. The sides of the muscular foot have fine threads which are the snail's sense organs. Top shells are vegetarians, and take in their tiny food with the radula, with its delicate teeth.

One of the poisonous snails, also rare on the beach, though it lives in shallow water, is the alphabet cone. Its shell is sharp-pointed at the top, slim at the bottom, cream-white with irregular golden mottling. It is ornamental and looks manmade, and the spots could be a code in a strange language. The animal has a coiled poison duct, which discharges a few drops at a time onto a kind of harpoon which is actually a tooth. The alphabet cone's tooth injects the poison into its victims, usually marine worms, though it will occasionally spear a fish. The apparatus is also used in defense against octopuses, which eat mollusks. Some of the Pacific varieties of cone actually can sting and even kill human beings. The Sanibel alphabet cone is not so dangerous, though we would not like to pick up a live one. Empty, on the beach, they are smooth as shining porcelain.

The octopuses, which eat cones as well as clams and crabs or indeed any live meat to be found in the ocean, are sometimes found small and young in shallow water along the beach. If you find one, beware. They bite. They have a parrot-like beak, and teeth. Even a small one can give a nasty slash to the hand that is trying to put it in a formaldehyde bottle. If you succeed in getting it before it gets you, you will find many facets of this highest class of mollusk that set it apart from all others. It has no outside shell; it has a real brain, large, perfect eyes, two kidneys, three hearts and blue blood. The blood is blue not on account of its proud family history but because it is a cold-blooded animal, and cold blood is blue. Two hundred million years ago it dominated the ocean, and even now it is an animal to be reckoned with, the Atlantic variety having arms three feet long and a weight of about twenty pounds. The largest, in the Pacific, has a spread of thirty-two feet and weighs up to one hundred and ten pounds. The thin rubbery arms radiating from the soft amorphous body, distinguished only by the extraordinary eyes and the gape of mouth, give the animal a fiendish appearance. It does not look at all like a mollusk. It swims with its eight arms streaming behind it, or walks on the bottom, occasionally grasping a victim, to enclose it, bite it and suck it in alive. The female lays clusters of long eggs, which she guards, cleans and caresses (to aerate them) until they hatch.

A delicate, thin-walled mollusk is the fig, a rounded snail, whitish with tinges of pink or pale brown, so it looks as though it were blushing. It gets to be about ten inches long, and the body, as with many gastropods, comes out all over the shell, spotted brown. It is an enormous body for such a frail shell, but when necessary it contracts all the way in so it cannot be seen. We found them common, but they are rarely found anywhere but the west coast of Florida, where they live in sand and eat sea urchins.

Murex shells come in many guises, but they are all heavily ridged, and some have thin spines all over, like a covering of lace. These snails are fiercely carnivorous and can force open the toughest clam or oyster. To do this they thrust a muscled foot at the clam and suck it apart, at the same time prying at it with the strong, sharp outer lip, and tearing the flesh with the radula. Murexes had a use for the Phoenicians and Romans, a gland that produces a yellowish fluid. This turns purple in sunny air, and was used as a dye for state robes. Probably its use to the snail is to anesthetize its prey. It has a horrible smell, but evidently the ancients didn't mind it.

The loveliest, most appealing shell of all is the lady's ear. It is a small flattened snail, white as the beach, and it looks like any number of ordinary bleached shells. But it is born white, with fine lines around its low top, and its inside shines. When alive it is not appealing at all, being a close relative of the destructive moon snail that decimates clam and oyster beds. Its body is a gelatinous mass, the color of wet sand, covering the entire shell, and it is found by its slow track along the lower beach at very low tide. It is a wonder that it can retreat into its interior, which is almost nonexistent. Retreat it does, though. Most marine snails have bodies out of

all proportion to their shells. When you pick up a lady's ear
alive the body retracts so that all of it lies almost invisible
against the open interior. Snails are elastic, and that is what
keeps them alive. When feeding they can spread widely, and
when frightened or exposed to air they can become small vis-
cous bodies protecting themselves far within their shells.

6.

*T*here are a number of animals besides mollusks on the beach. The horseshoe crab, which looks like an enormous beetle with a long thin tail, is not a crustacean like other crabs, but is the only marine relative of the scorpions and spiders. It grows up to twenty inches in diameter, and despite its fearsome appearance, is not dangerous. It lives in quiet waters, just below tide line, buried in the sand, and is occasionally stranded on the beach after a particularly low tide. It is descended almost unchanged from ancestors of Cambrian times, about 500 million years ago; and its forebears, trilobites, are among the oldest fossils. The life of this ancient creature is quiet; it eats worms and other small marine animals, staying mostly where it started as an adult. The female horseshoe crab lays her eggs in the sand where she lives, and the young, when hatched, disappear into deeper water until their shells have grown and hardened. The adult has a vast expanse of horny back shell which serves as protection against other animals and as a device for keeping the creature right side up in rough tides, and four pairs of spiderlike legs on the under side. There is no visible head or mouth. The slender tail spine is not used for attack but as a lever. When the crab is turned over it pushes the tip into the sand and, if lucky, flips back. If the sand shifts too much in a strong tide the device does not work and the animal is doomed. Those so numerous on the beach are not live horseshoe crabs but the shed shells of larger ones still in the water. As the animal grows it discards the smaller shells, and they close up, looking as if they were still alive, and wash up on the beach. An awkward animal it is, underdeveloped and antediluvian, obviously a living fossil. Its main interest is that it is one of the oldest forms of animal life in the world, and is rapidly diminishing because of its frequent use in fertilizers. When you see numbers of the shells stranded, dark brown, on the white sand, you could be back there, with the first life on a stark earth.

Once we saw an oyster catcher, all by itself. It is a beach bird, and lives on the mollusk that gives it its name. Heavyset, black and white, it has a long red bill, flattened vertically so it can prise its shell food open like an expert in a fish market. The few shy couples to be found are always together, and altogether it is rare in North America. This one looked abandoned, a lonely straggler on a strange beach. We circled it at a distance, but a group of shell collectors approached too close and the bird flew, to land farther up the beach, still alone.

One day we saw a strange fish gasping at the edge of the waterline. It was a cowfish, turquoise in color with gold flecks, not unlike the water of the Gulf, and flat-bottomed, with a triangular shape, sharp at the top. I picked it up and found it had, not scales, but a sort of shell, with winglike fins and eyes at the sides of the head. It was probably very comfortable sitting at the bottom of the sea, able to see backwards, forwards and sideways, well armored and protectively colored to match the water and the bottom grass in which it had lived. The earliest skeletons of sea animals were on the outside rather than the inside, and the cowfish still wears its skeleton that way. The color varies according to the fish's habitat. Some find themselves born on sand, and they are mottled brownish, others on underwater rocks, where they take on the mixed gray of their surroundings. It looked remarkably out of place, bright-colored and helpless, on the sun-drenched sand.

Far out in the Gulf late one afternoon, we saw a flash of silver, then another and another. The exhibition lasted well into sunset. Tarpon generally roll on the surface, but these were leaping up as they do when they are hooked, and diving under again with a flick of the big bright tail. Whether they were playing, like dolphins, or whether this was a method of food gathering was not clear. There must have been three or four dozen in the group, and they were there very early in the year. Tarpon do not usually appear in numbers until late spring and summer. This was mid-March. No one knows where they spend their youth. No tarpon under a foot long has ever been sighted or hooked. The adults live along the coasts of Central America and the Carribbean Islands and come north with warm weather to spawn off the west coast of Florida.

A friend who is an ardent deep-sea sports fisherman suggested that we go out the next morning. Sanibel is neither a fishing nor a sailing resort, its inhabitants being more interested in shells and birds, so we located a fishing guide at Fort Myers Beach, Captain Buck Fernandez. He came the next morning in his comfortable little boat, set up for deep-sea fishing, and picked us up at Bailey's Dock, where the mail boat used to land. Captain Buck is a pleasant-looking, soft-spoken Floridian, probably descended from Portuguese fishermen of the same name who came to Fort Myers Beach in the late nineteenth century. He knows his fish, and though he did not then have sonar he had a knack for finding fish that brought other boats in his wake. We cruised up the bay shore, well out from land, in the only channel for boats, marked by tall heavy posts with numbers painted on them. The Gulf was reached through Redfish Pass, between Captiva and Upper Captiva. We trolled slowly up and down the shore of Sanibel. Out in the open sea the sun was brilliant and dangerous. We were covered from head to foot for protection; any exposed spot would get painfully burned. The Gulf was like glass, and the long bright day made us sleepy. About noon I hooked something and immediately saw it rise and dive in a simulation of the tail dance we had seen the evening before. The captain and others offered to help me bring it in. I declined. Only once in my life before this had I caught a fish: I hooked a small trout on a worm, probably by mistake, in a New Jersey pond. Now I wanted to see what would happen between me and this big fish. It was a forty-five-minute struggle, and the tarpon was courageous. He jumped out of the water again and again, trying to loosen the hook. Since his jaw is heavily plated with bone, and I had hooked him not in the mouth but under the chin, this should have been a simple matter. But each time he soared I tightened the line. He tried sounding and the line sped out of the reel. But by this time he was tired, and I brought him slowly to the side of the boat. There he rolled and tried to jump again, but finally he was still. The captain reached over with his gaff hook but I wanted to let the fish go. He had fought well and long, with great spirit, and he wasn't even bleeding. He would live many more years with the small scar of the hook under his jaw. Captain Buck is not a callous fisherman, but if I didn't want the fish he did. It was the first tarpon caught that season, and he wanted to show that it had been caught from his boat, a form of advertising with which one cannot argue. He gaffed the fish through the gill and brought it on deck. Its back was blue-gray, shading into shining silver on the sides, and its mouth was large, with an out-jutting lower jaw that looked like stone. That it had been hooked at all, much less stayed hooked and landed, was hardly believable. This tough and beautiful animal changed my mind about fishing at once. No other was caught that day, though some rolled in the distance. We went back to Bailey's Dock in the late afternoon and I carried the fish ashore. As I stood on the dock, the fish hanging from the gaff hook, as tall as my shoulder, a small white cat came from nowhere and purred, licking the tarpon's tail and rubbing gently against it. It was not a greedy cat but a happy one; it liked having a tarpon to caress.

The fish has been stuffed in the position the fisherman is familiar with, head high, body arched, tail flipped upward. The only mark is that of the gaff hook, where the blood was washed off and the wound repaired. It looks like a model of a tarpon. I should have let the captain have it.

We went fishing with Captain Buck a few other times, but the tarpon were not running, which was as well, for I did not want to catch another. In fact, in March almost nothing is running. We ran into a throng of grouper on a submerged reef, idling sluggishly. They don't fight; you just haul them up, once in a while losing the hook in a rock crevice. They are found only by sonar, as they don't move much from their hiding places. No silver tail-dancing fish this, but a large edible sea bass, dark brown and mottled with dark gray. The captain sold them from his dock at Fort Myers Beach.

Another time we found a school of mackerel, light blue and yellow-spotted, beautiful fish, game fighters and good eating. They did not present much difficulty because they were small. As we trolled a large shadow appeared in the water near the surface. It was a good deal larger than the boat, and we immediately reeled in, as Captain Buck speeded up the engine to get as far away as possible. It was a whale shark, the largest fish known, weighing up to fifteen tons. It is not in the least dangerous, living near the surface to feed on small sea animals, which it strains in the manner of baleen whales. While it would not have taken our hooks it might inadvertently have toppled the boat.

The Gulf is a peaceful body of water in general, and on our few trips we had many hours to survey the smooth surface with land only a low line of beaches and mangroves, not far away but unidentifiable. Out on the water brown pelicans were the liveliest sight, though they were not often conspicuously active. Other than observing pelicans there is not much to do. A real sportsman would find our slow trolling almost illegitimate and certainly dull. But it gives time for thought, and where in the world, doing what, does one find that? The occasional fish hooked keeps us just busy enough. The sun is hot, the water is bright, life is empty of complications. One cannot do this every day, but once in a while it purifies the mind.

Though Sanibel residents seldom fish from boats, many cast their lines from the beach. They catch little, but they are determined, and will fish for hours. They bring in sea trout, an ordinary-looking but tasty fish, and once in a while a shark. We saw a hammerhead that had been hooked and left to die on the beach by a disgusted and frightened beach caster. The fisherman had cut his line well away from the dangerous teeth that are under the chin, hidden by the snout. Actually neither chin nor snout are visible. The skull is extended horizontal to the body and flattened at the squared corners. At these corners are its eyes, so it can see behind as well as ahead. The hammerhead shark misses little. The one we saw was only about eighteen inches long, but a one hundred fifty pounder was caught in the bay, and they can grow to more than one thousand pounds and over twelve feet. It is generally believed that where there are dolphins there are no sharks. The dolphins destroy the sharks, which would otherwise devour their young, butting their heavy heads into fish much larger then they. Dead sharks have been found with big holes in their sides.

However, though there are great numbers of dolphins in the waters around Sanibel, there are still sharks. When, on a moonlight swim, you see a dark fin cutting the water, you cannot be sure, and the moonlight swim, however cool and beautiful, ends with quiet abruptness. No one says anything; all just retreat, to watch the silver water from the sand and wonder what was out there so sinister or probably so harmless. Black-bellied plovers whistle around us in the darkness, their voices plaintive. The beach is theirs at night. It is plain that we are not wanted, either in the water or on the sand.

7.

*T*hough we were often on the water, as Sanibel lures its visitors out to the calm sea, the island itself is endlessly fascinating to us. The beaches are seldom crowded, and very few tourists are interested in the flat, low-treed interior of the island in March. There are little things to see, though. A pileated woodpecker works on the wall of the church, for the sake of carpenter ants or beetle larvae. They say it always starts tapping like a loud hammer when the minister begins his sermon. The minister is deaf but his congregation is not. A pair of pileated woodpeckers nested for years next to our hotel, and another in a hole of a telephone post. In fact they used to be common on Sanibel. One rarely sees them now because most of their favored tall trees have been destroyed, either by human builders or by the large holes drilled by the woodpeckers themselves. They have the distinction of being the largest of the North American woodpeckers, as well as the noisiest, with the exception of the ivory-billed, now nearly or possibly already completely extinct. The pileated woodpeckers' hammering sounds like the blows of an ax. With the deep black of back and sharp white of wings and neck and the large bright red crest, they are not easy to miss.

A commoner, smaller woodpecker is the red-bellied — misnamed, as the belly is the only part that is not gaudy. It too is a continual noisemaker, not so much by its excavating activities as by its loud, frequent and nonmusical calls. In contrast to most others of its family it eats largely vegetable matter. It does not shun human company; in fact, it appears to be trying to annihilate the cottages of our hotel. When not working fruitlessly on the walls it digs into rotting coconuts under the floors, possibly to get nourishment to continue its wrecking operations.

On the lawns behind the hotel, cattle egrets pick in the ground for insects. For a heron this is a squat bird, unusually tame. It came from Africa, in the late nineteenth century, making its way from Dakar to the nearest point on South America, probably Natal or Recife in Brazil, with the help of the strong winds of the South Atlantic. The cattle egret found the western hemisphere delightful; the birds had not been in Brazil very long before they were found breeding in southern Florida, and by now they have increased enormously. There are no horses or cattle on Sanibel, but there are plenty of insects. Their habit in Africa was to follow grazing animals and pluck the insects from the dung. Here they don't have to follow anything, but placidly walk around the grass, where the food is, not looking at their observers. They are white, but not pure white, and lack the delicate plumes of the snowy egret, which they somewhat resemble. There is a coarse crest, raised in the nuptial season, and visible at close range at other times like a stain of dried blood from the yellowish beak to the back of the neck. They are comfortable birds, and it is good to know that they like us, or at least our country, in spite of being outsiders.

Going down the middle of the island, overgrown with low palmetto, one is never bored. A pair of eagles and a pair of ospreys alternated years in the same nest on a telephone post. The post came down in a hurricane and the eagles and ospreys took off for less inhabited parts of the island. Very common still are meadowlarks and mockingbirds, and their songs follow us everywhere. Turkey vultures and black vultures circle continually, and every half mile or so on the main road we come upon a kestrel perched on the power wire, that darts off as we come near. It is a handsome little hawk, by far the most numerous of its family on the island. While other hawks, eagles and ospreys grow fewer each year the kestrel remains populous. It dives gracefully or hovers like a hummingbird over the coarse grass, keeping on one place with strong quick wing beats. A red-shouldered hawk quartered a flat grassy section with bedraggled cabbage palms in it, and dodged from one palm to the other as we walked through his hunting ground. The palms have been cut down now for a new development, and as with the eagles and ospreys the hawks have moved to inaccessible places.

At the southern end of the island is the Sanibel lighthouse, with a beautiful small sanctuary behind it. The woods have been left, untouched by farmers or developers, and they are surprisingly deep and tall. Though there are birds there too, mostly wintering warblers and vireos, it is the vegetation that holds the interest. Poinsettias grow unchecked, much smaller than their Mexican relatives. The green leaves are slender, with splashes of red on the top ones. The actual flower is hardly visible, a cluster of small yellow blooms. The bright red on the top leaves serves to attract insects for pollination. Coconuts are in bloom, their long slim golden flowers cascading from the center of the crown, and beneath them are new small coconuts, the same color. Cabbage palms, almost the symbol of Florida, rear shaggy heads from a straight height of forty to fifty feet. The top fronds are green with feathered ends; the lower droop brownly down the trunk. Some of the old fronds become attached to the tree, as in all palms; most hang loose in ragged strands that rustle at the least breeze. Strangler figs like the straight stems of the cabbage palms. Their seeds, indigestible to birds, are dropped intact from a flying bird to the head of the palm, and there they germinate. The young plant sends roots down around the trunk in a heavy gray lattice. Reaching the earth, they spread in a large area around the palm, often showing above ground. They do not literally strangle the tree, but they often grow so big that their leaves shade the palm fronds and their host dies from lack of sun. This is the way this fig lives, and when you see, as you often do, a full fig tree with no sign of root lattice or host, you know that inside that strong gray trunk are the rotting remains of a cabbage palm, immolated in a living coffin.

We could not stray off the path because poison ivy is thick. It grows all through the island except near the beaches, where salt wind would kill it. In it and above it are the small birds that find attractive the dense vegetation and the stream that parallels the trail. A white-eyed vireo sang suddenly and startlingly a few feet from us. Yellow-throated warbler, parula and others added their short high songs. It is a beautiful stretch of wilderness, a little piece of interior Sanibel as it probably all used to be.

At the end of the Lighthouse walk, in an open area, grows a small tropical tree called the orchid tree. It was brought from India, but does very well in this semitropical setting. There are many on Sanibel, growing as high as thirty-five feet, with fat little two-lobed leaves and, in winter and spring, an abundance of large pale purple, pink and white blossoms so much like orchids that at first they seem to be orchid plants growing on the branches.

The trail ends in a sand road, and from there we walked down to the edge of the bay. There was a warm tidal pool on the flat sandy beach, almost uninhabited. Probably the bay water seldom came up that far, and whatever remained was eaten by shorebirds and gulls. One sign of life was a red worm, about an inch long, flattened and thin. It swam around the edges of its pool contentedly, feeding on minute algae. We fished it out with a twig and it immediately contracted, drawing its broad head and bluntly pointed tail as close together as possible. It was a ribbon worm, dangerous to no one, as it is not a parasite, and it can grow over ninety feet long. Scientists who have found and measured the animal must find it, if not frightening, at least interesting to see a skinny scarlet worm that long. We put it back in its home, to give it a chance to put on a few more inches. It would not grow even that, however. It is a wonder it was there at all. The edges of the shallow pool were crisscrossed with the claw marks of birds, and as soon as we left they would come back and pick out the little worm much more easily than we had.

Shell gatherers used to walk around the lighthouse and

A strangler fig encloses a live cabbage palm. The network of roots will grow into a solid trunk, and the palm inside will die from lack of air.

pick up astounding shells. When we first visited the island we were shown Scotch bonnets and junonias that had been found on that point. Something must have happened to the currents, for now the beach is a mass of unidentifiable fragments. In fact it has very nearly been reduced to sand, the fine clinging white sand that is made of shells.

8.

*A*t the northwestern end of Sanibel is the widest part of the Gulf beach. In back of it is Blind Pass, the water corridor between Captiva and Sanibel. Originally it was a blind pass, the bay water coming slowly to a shallow halt between the two islands. When we first knew the island, however, hurricanes had broken the barrier, and Blind Pass poured into the Gulf, deep and swift. There were the anglers with their worms and shrimps. There also, on the sharp point of sand on the Captiva side, were black skimmers and royal terns and ring-billed and laughing gulls, resting on their bellies. They were streamlined, beaks pointing into the Gulf wind, tails long and straight behind, as if the continuous airflow had shaped them so. Now Blind Pass has closed up again, and the skimmers and terns have gone somewhere else for their naps. Still there, in the migration season, are myriads of small shorebirds. They arrive unevenly: one day there will be a flock of Cuban plovers, little and pale as the sand, almost invisible on the upper part of the beach; the next day they will be gone and in their stead are sandpipers of many kinds, all looking alike. Sorting them out is a long process, and we go through it every year. It is particularly difficult because they are constantly on the move, whirring over sand and water, to alight for a few minutes, then take off again.

It is a good beach for small mollusks, and that is probably why the shorebirds gather in such quantities. Wentletraps, pure white, ribbed snails not over an inch long, look as if they are made of the most delicate china; the name is Swedish for spiral staircase. The animal in this beautiful shell feeds voraciously on sea anemones much larger than itself. It will attack anything else if it cannot find sea anemones. In the same aquarium where the little skate lived briefly a live nutmeg had a temporary home. It is a demure marine snail, light brown and thin-shelled. The aquarium's owner dropped in a wentletrap. Within seconds the small white snail had attached itself to the nutmeg, about four times its size, in preparation to drill. It was not easy to pluck off. We don't know what happened to them after that. Presumably they were both put back in the Gulf, to forage unmolested.

Ivory tusk shells, which belong to one of the five classes of mollusks, shine in the sand. This species, which prefers shallow, sandy water, can grow as long as two and one half inches, but those carried up on the beach by the Gulf's slow tide are

The wide beach at Blind Pass is a favored place for shore birds. Small mollusks abound, and a heron finds its food exposed at low water line.

usually only about one half inch, narrow and fragile. It is a primitive mollusk, without head, eyes, gills or hearts. A larger form lives off the Pacific coast, and was used by the Indians of the Northwest as wampum. The food of the Sanibel variety is a one-celled marine animal with a shell, called foraminifera, which is crushed by the small animal's razorlike teeth.

Coffee beans, half-inch long brown cowries belonging to the class of Gastropoda (most of which are snails), are strewn over the beach, smooth, spotted and glossy. It is not known on what they feed, but the presumption is that hydroids and related small invertebrates sustain them. If that is so the coffee bean does not have to range far for its food. Hydroids, feathery colonies that look like rose-colored ferns, are attached to wharf pilings or breakwaters along the coast. They set free small swimming jellyfish by the hundred, which are swept out to sea by the tide. The jellyfish drift and grow all winter, then send out their seed as hydroids, which drift back inshore again, to form new colonies.

Horn shells, brown and gray, are usually about one half inch long. They are narrow snails that live in shallow warm water and are picked up at low tide by the feeding sandpipers. Their own food is detritus, so they serve a double purpose: to keep their areas clean and, after this is done, to be eaten. They used to be the main food of the flamingoes when, in Audubon's time, flamingoes still existed in great numbers all along the southern Gulf coast.

The worm shell is another snail common on the wide beach. It is loosely spiraled, with a neat sharp point at the end of the uneven curves, and, when alive, leads a soft life inside a sponge. It looks remarkably like a calcified worm, and some recoil at the sight of it.

An odd little snail is the simnia, which has a slim shiny shell and lives on sea whips, delicately branched algae. Its color depends on the color of its home, purple or yellow, and it is extremely difficult to see, being about the same width as the thin frond of the seaweed. It feeds on polyps, almost invisible animals that also inhabit sea whips.

The big beach is immensely populated, and one can spend hours there, chasing sandpipers, walking quietly up to the little tame plovers, or just sitting on the sand sifting handfuls of shells or watching a gull soar up and drop a little clam to get at the morsel inside. The empty shells give massive evidence of the life in the sea, and even so they are a microscopic portion of marine animal life. It has been estimated that there are about 34 billion tons of this life, twenty times the seas' total plants, which are 1.7 billion tons. It appears odd that the marine animal population is so much bigger than the plant, unlike the ratio on the land masses. Probably the reason is the short life of the oceanic plant and the relatively long life of the animals. We could harvest enough from the seas to feed the biggest human population. As of now we use about 60 million tons of fish each year, but if existing ships and nets and lines were used more carefully and thoroughly we could have thirty times as much. We have a long way to go in this field, and, having more or less used up our earth resources, we may come to depend on the ocean. It is to be hoped that we don't destroy its life before we need it. Nuclear bombs under water and oil slicks on the surface are only two of the ways in which the ocean is already being rendered uninhabitable.

9.

*B*lind Pass itself has not nearly so much life, but one can launch a canoe there, near the bridge between Sanibel and Captiva. Along the sides of the pass are mangroves dusted with white where pelicans have roosted, and a number of herons hide among the twisted roots looking like mangrove trunks themselves, thin-necked and gray in the shadows. On the inland shore there are a few new houses, comfortable-looking and well built, with big picture windows or glassed-in porches. Living in them, however, must be a permanent arrangement. Though the view is pleasant the mosquitoes are thick, and there is no real ground underfoot, just the mud made by mangroves. All the inhabitants can do is sit at their picture windows and look out. The inland water parts of Sanibel are altogether favorable to mosquitoes. One night a single mosquito trap under a sea grape caught 365,696 mosquitoes, a world record. Salt marsh mosquito eggs have been counted as high as 45,000 per square foot, or two billion to an acre. We did not envy the people their bright new houses on Blind Pass.

Soon the pass widens into an inland bay, Clam Bayou, with side arms in every direction, some leading into blind alleys, some expanding into still other large inland bays. It is a deserted area from start to finish. No one can build there, and the only sign of human life was an abandoned houseboat. A great deal of water takes up the northern side of Sanibel, unseen and mostly unguessed, hiding among its low forests. These bays are the haunts of bald eagles and ospreys and red-shouldered hawks. Here they can nest safely and fish the quiet water, so clear one can see the crown conches crawling on the bottom, bristly snails gray with mud and algae. Crown conches are beautiful when cleaned. They look like elegant chess pieces, streaked brown, with a row of sharp, curved spines just below the top whorl.

Even here in the windless inland bay not all is peace. The five ospreys we saw, two on a nest, were readily aggressive, not to us but to the eagles, which were apparently disturbed by everything. A pair of eagles soared almost together out of the sky and landed on a mangrove, to perch quietly within a few feet of each other. Out of nowhere a red-shouldered hawk dived at them. Perhaps it had a nest nearby — the aggressor is usually the one who has the near nest. The hawk was much smaller, but more than a match for the eagles. The hawk gave a screaming whistle and the eagles flew away again. Another eagle, alone, caught a fish and circled around the area of an osprey's occupied nest, apparently not knowing what to do. It finally settled just behind the nest, the fish still in its talons. Perhaps the ospreys had taken over its nest. We have seen them do this easily and often.

There is one woman who knows Sanibel's inland water, and takes fishing parties into the bayous when the wind is too sharp outside. That is Lorraine Woodring, who came here from Cuba in the early 1920's and stayed to become a symbol of the island. We never went fishing with her, but once she took us across Pine Island Sound to a small mangrove island with a shallow harbor. It is a magnificent roosting place for wood ibis, white ibis, pelicans and the supreme frigate bird, which we see occasionally high in the sky, an attenuated coal-black cross. The seven-foot wings, thin and tapered, are crooked at the elbow, the scissor tail is usually folded, and the bird appears not to move. Suddenly he dips his long neck, folds his wings and hurtles toward the water. Inches above it he extends his wings again, opens his hooked beak and seizes a surface-feeding fish. He cannot land in the water, as his feathers are not adapted. Up he goes again, soaring to great heights without moving a wing. He weighs only about three pounds, so, with his great wings, he floats easily in the upper air. Perched there on the tops of the mangroves he is equally impressive. His throat has swollen into a crimson balloon, as it is the breeding season and he intends to attract a mate. He may already have one; often frigate birds keep the bright pouch expanded through nesting time, as a deterrent to other birds.

On the way back, in a sunset as bright as the frigate bird's neck, Lorraine pointed to a ripple at the surface. It was a log-gerhead turtle coming up to breathe, and the size of its back shell could be seen, about three feet long. These reptiles were land-based for more than 200 million years, and took to the sea only when they were pushed off by the first population explosion of warm-blooded hairy mammals, about 60 million years ago. They still lay their eggs on land, on southern beaches, and used to be numerous on Sanibel and Captiva, with about two thousand nests during the breeding season. The huge turtles, which can weigh up to four hundred and fifty pounds, clamber up the beach during the night from May to August, for three nesting times, with eighty to one hundred and fifty round white soft eggs each time. Only the female comes out of the water, the male hovering below, close to the shoreline, while she is pursuing her clandestine, dangerous operation. She digs the nest with her flippers (the bones of which, when scales and flesh are stripped, are recognizable as arms and legs much like ours). After excavating a hole about two feet deep and eight inches in diameter, she turns around and drops the eggs in one by one, each coated with protective mucus. The well-known weeping turtle is a female covering the nest and spraying sand over and around it until its location is undetectable. The tears are produced by glands near the eyes, and wash the sand out. Well might she weep. On Sanibel the turtle nests have been almost totally destroyed. There used to be an abnormally high raccoon population; the animals gathered in family groups and plucked the eggs from the sand while the mother turtle was still dropping them into the nest. In 1964 a virus infection nearly eliminated the raccoons, but the turtle nests continued to be depredated. Sand crabs, which had been a favorite food of raccoons, increased enormously. The sand crab, or ghost crab, the color of the dry sand it lives in and almost invisible, inhabits the same area as the turtle nest, between normal high tide and vegetation line. Like the fiddler crab, which it resembles, it burrows into the sand, and can tunnel directly into the nests to devour the turtle eggs, which are about its own size.

The loggerhead has plant enemies as well. While she excavates she is likely to cut through the roots of sea oats. The roots grow again, and become so matted that the hatchlings cannot escape, and die in the nest.

In addition to plants and wild animals, hurricanes bring high tides to wash out the nest. And no one can eliminate that careless destroyer, man. Adult turtle meat may not taste good, but it is nevertheless eaten. Eggs are taken for food or fun. It must be irresistible for children and some adults to walk the beaches at night and find the great reptiles dedicated to their task, mark the spot and go back later to remove the eggs. The adult turtles themselves have few enemies. Shrimp boats are a menace, and turtles sometimes become entangled in the trawls and drown; besides that there is an occasional turtle hunter, who works with a spear.

In spite of its awesome appearance the loggerhead does not attack any large animal unless it is frightened. It has no teeth, but a horny beak. It prefers hermit crabs, shellfish, which it opens with the beak, and Portuguese men of war; it is one of the few creatures that can eat this poisonous jellyfish. Its scales protect it from the stings, but it has to close its eyes.

The gentleness of the loggerhead and the extreme vulnerability of eggs and hatchlings make one wonder how it has survived at all through these millions of years. It has been estimated that of about six thousand hatchlings that reach the sea in one year on Sanibel, perhaps fifteen will live to breed, coming back to the ancestral beaches six to ten years later. No one knows where they are once the young swim out to sea. Now they are protected on the island, and it is unlawful to bother females coming up to lay their eggs, or to handle the eggs or disturb the nest in any way. However, it is impossible to patrol all the beaches every night during the laying, and the loggerhead population is still diminishing. There is a turtle hatchery by the lighthouse, where eggs collected by officials of the Fish and Wildlife Service and the Conservation Foundation were buried in soft sand and protected from predators by close wiring. In 1970, 5,500 hatched, and the young turtles, about five inches long, were removed to a sanctuary at Tarpon Bay. There they lived, crowded into aquariums, fed on fish donated by the island's anglers, until they were large enough to be safely released into the Gulf. When we saw them they seemed to be covered with dark algae, but they were lively enough. Perhaps, on Sanibel at least, the loggerheads will be brought back to a safe number.

For years loggerheads provided Lorraine with a small but lucrative business. She could sell the meat to the poor people of the island, and the shell is precious. She carried a spear in her small boat always, and when a turtle showed its head she threw it. She seldom missed. When she did she steered her boat where she knew by experience it would come up again, then leaped on its wide back, to kill it with another thrust of the spear. Lorraine has a strong, expressionless face, but when she laughed, as she did in describing the hunt, she was beautiful. Her own skill provided her with infectious joy. She hunts no longer, as she is scrupulous in observing the law, and the stern face seldom relaxes. She does not have an easy life.

Lorraine lives in an old house on the bay side of the island. Its backyard is a curious litter. Old car parts alternate with large tropical flowering plants. She bought them small-sized in little pots on the mainland and put them in her yard, where the steamy heat encouraged them to their native growth. In front are her own dock and her own boat, neatly kept, and back of the yard is a shed which is not neatly kept, bearing

243

the overflow of children and grandchildren. She proposed an oyster roast in the shed. She tore off mangrove branches with the little oysters that line it, shoved back the children's outgrown playthings, put up a rickety table and started a fire in front of the shed. The picnic had not a prepossessing appearance when we arrived. It was raining slightly, mosquitoes abounded except near the smoky fire, and the shed and the table looked old and worn and ready to fall down. There were eight of us, some young, some old, and there was no reason we should be gathered at this unlikely place. All this changed imperceptibly as Lorraine thrust the mangrove sticks into the low fire and handed them to us a few minutes later. There is nothing sweeter than a mangrove oyster, and we ate them right off the branches. We forgot the mosquitoes, the rain stopped, and Lorraine wanted us to be happy. She knows her Sanibel, and she made us see it in her light. The tropical plants were unbelievably lush in her disorderly garden, and the spirit of friendliness grew among us in the same way — the way of island life on the back coast.

Wandering along the narrow beach beside her dock we found many of the fragile clams called rose petals. Among them were pointed Venus clams, white, with subtle shading of brown or black along the hinge, looking much like the sand they inhabited, and shaped by the water into tapered ends and rounded valves, perfect small sea gems. Rose petals and Venus clams are there no longer, and the mangrove oysters have been polluted by chemical fertilizer flowing out through the Caloosahatchee River. There used to be dozens of snowy egrets, fishing from the beach. They are not there now, shunning the polluted water, though the island supports many hundreds of these birds, along the new canals and in the big sanctuary. Lorraine's activities have been curtailed to guiding fishermen in the bay. The shed has not yet fallen down but it is even more lopsided than when we ate oysters there, and the junk has accumulated. Still she lives on, a straight and proud old woman, part of the island as it used to be.

Across the island from Lorraine Woodring's house, on the Gulf shore, is another bit of unchanged Sanibel. A couple, Mr. and Mrs. Willis Combs, have retired, built a beautiful, simple house, and left their small lot untouched. All the native Sanibel vegetation is there, more than three hundred species, including, as at Lorraine's, tropical plants that have sprung up to be the giants they should be. The most striking is a split-leaved philodendron they planted near a tall cabbage palm. It uses the palm — most of these imported plants are lianas — and has grown up and around it, dropping its ropes to the ground in typical jungle fashion.

The strangest plant on the Combs' land is *Psilotum nudum,* sometimes known as whisk fern. It is not a fern, being far older in its land history; the first plant on land to stand upright, with its own shadow behind it. It has no root, but must have its existence in a specialized environment. It has to be part underground, needs some sun and some shade, and particularizes in the areas around cabbage palms, where there is likely to be plenty of moisture and humus. It probably came out of the sea in the early Devonian period, about 400 million years ago, and has survived exactly in its ancient form. It has been found in fossil shape dating back to that period, and that it is still around is somewhat a miracle. It does not look like much, a thin stem bearing a few even thinner branches, no leaves or flowers, but spores for reproduction. The whole thing is not more than four inches high and extremely frail-looking. However it is the prize plant of the Combs' native garden. A bulldozer came as far as the turnaround before their house, intending to tear through a right-of-way. Down

245

*Sea grapes as old as a hundred years grow in the Combs'
garden, their flowers bright yellow against the sand. The
fruit was eaten by the Caloosas, and Spanish explorers used
the leathery leaves as stationery.*

would have gone the cabbage palm and its rare little neighbor. Mr. Combs stood in front of the machine, presumably to dare his life to spare the fossil plant. The bulldozer went no farther, and since then a zoning ordinance was declared covering his land. On his property, as on most of the Gulf frontage, are sea grapes, and when we first saw these beautiful spreading trees they were just in flower, large blossoms, light yellow, with five overlapping petals. Later they deepened to yellow-orange, and when they began to die were dark red with yellow shadings. A flower for a florist's shop, one would think, but on Sanibel they are common, like the brilliant red hibiscus and the purple flow of bougainvillea. All of these would be endangered by severe frost, but the light frosts of Sanibel do not bother them.

Wild coffee lines the driveway, shaded by cabbage palms or gumbo-limbo trees. It is native to Sanibel, though coffee trees are usually associated with the hot humid lands of Java or Brazil. The shiny leaves are strongly ribbed, and here, in its wild state, it is no more than a shrub, growing thickly in a dense ornamental border.

Cat's-claw lives there, a shrub with clusters of little red leaves and thorns long and back-curved. Moses-in-the-bulrushes is a deep-red lily close to the ground. It has no stem and the flower is like a closed cradle among the long leaves. Banana trees, imported, produce minute bananas. The Mexican flame plant, a vine, has a scarlet bloom like a thin-petaled daisy. The Combs' garden is altogether a place to dream in, all year round. Just beyond it, over a slight rise, are the beach and the blue Gulf.

10.

*F*rom the Combs' beach it is not a long walk to the sandpipers' beach, and from there on to the coastline of Captiva,
at first barely differentiated from Sanibel's. The beach turns
north, and gradually differences become noticeable. The wind
and currents along Captiva's once wide beach have eroded it
so far that the coast road has been destroyed and sand piled
up to the very edge of the woods. The inhabitants of the lovely
old houses now look out only on debris, with the water racing
along the edge. Every time a storm comes a little more is

gone, and it is likely that eventually there will be no Captiva, only the sand ridge which was its predecessor.

Whenever we go that way we look for an eagle's nest which has been there for many years. It is in the top of an Australian pine, a bundle of sticks growing from year to year, usually with the white head of an eagle visible over the edge, sometimes both eagles there, one perched very near the other. So far they have not been disturbed by ospreys, surprisingly. There is a pair of ospreys not far away which tried to build a nest. They abandoned it in the face of storms, leaving a few sticks untidily balanced in a fork of the dead tree. The next year they were back again, in the same place, with a whole nest and a full-sized set of anxiety symptoms. Their nest tree is on the very edge of Captiva's only road, and everyone traveling that way stops to stare, photograph and admire. The ospreys circle around their visitors keening sharply, almost attacking but not quite. We are too big, not like eagles. One of the ospreys almost always has a fish in its talons, but they never seem to take time to eat. Since they breed in the tourist season it is unlikely that these roadside eggs will hatch. Rarely one goes back to the nest to warm the eggs for a few minutes, but it is soon off again, worrying. There is little time for incubating, and the March air is cold.

At the northern end of Captiva is a vast hotel, the largest on the twin islands. One can rent a boat there, and cross Redfish Pass, a continually rippled, sometimes impassable rush of water, to the calm bay side of Upper Captiva. This little island suffers too from the invasion of water, and it is impossible to build there, as the tide sweeps from Gulf to bay at every hurricane. The only habitations are a small cluster of fishermen's houses at the northern tip, separated from the rest of the island by impenetrable mangrove forest. They are built on long stakes out into the water, and can be approached only by boat.

To walk on this deserted bit of Florida real estate is a wonderful experience. When you beach the boat you cross a mud flat, where thousands of fiddler crabs scurry before you into their holes, rustling like dry leaves. You reach a mangrove area which separates the bay from the Gulf, with its graceful Australian pines. Mangroves do not grow thickly on the southern part of Upper Captiva, as it is barely above high tide level and nothing can grow here very long. Still they have put down their long slender buttresses. The sand is loose and one can pull out a new root and examine its tentacles, curled and covered with sand like the fingers of a drowning body trying to cling to a sliding beach. Pulling up a mangrove root does not destroy it. As soon as it is dropped it falls to the same place, ready to dig in again. In the midst of the mangroves there is a little pool, and there sometimes is a reddish egret, fast-circling, like no other egret, to roil the water and bring little fish to the surface. They used to be much prized for their plumes, long and white at the tail, bronze-red on the head and neck, and they were almost extinct early in the twentieth century. Then wardens took over and the birds began to come back slowly. They are no longer a threatened species, though it is comparatively rare to see one among the mangroves. They apparently do better on the part of the Texas coast where almost the only vegetation is Spanish dagger and prickly pear.

There is an empty space between mangrove and Australian pine, bare sand and battered shells, where the water has rolled from time to time, and there we saw, extraordinarily, a colony of mushrooms on a bright dry day, small and brown and round-capped, like little people. They could almost have walked away. In fact maybe they did, as we never saw them again.

We walked up the center of the island through Australian

pines. Nothing grew beneath them, and it was like walking through a well-kept park. The water was visible on both sides, white-capped on the Gulf, calm and shallow on Pine Island Sound. The trees thinned and we came to a wide bay not more than two or three inches deep, through which we went bare-foot. Sandpipers and plovers fed there in great numbers, to fly only from our near footsteps and land immediately on a sand-spit, crying as they flew. Far out in the water was a colony of white pelicans, much larger than their brown relatives, nine-foot wings slightly raised so they looked like sailboats. They never dive for fish like brown pelicans, but thrash the water with their wings, startling up small fish. In a day they can eat up to a third of their weight, which is ordinarily about twenty pounds. Fresh water lakes in the northwest are their breeding places. In autumn they make a long diagonal migration south-east, ending in the shallow salt water where we saw them. In that colony was one great white heron, a rare bird seldom seen, standing tall, alone and aloof, as big as God, appar-ently with nothing to do. He had probably finished feeding, then spotted us and stood still, trusting that we would not see him. How could we miss?

At the end of the bay is a mangrove jungle, dark and heavy. Rather than go back through the bay and disturb its peaceful birds, we retreated to the middle of the narrow island, to the clear land beneath the Australian pines. On the occasional mangrove that survived in the deep shade were large colo-nies of periwinkles, a marine snail that has retreated almost entirely from its original home ground of the ocean, needing only an occasional wetting to keep it alive. Periwinkles are gradually becoming land snails, vegetarians, browsing off the small growths in their living area with the rasping tongue that is common to all snails. They hardly move, just enough to eat. We picked off a few, for the shells, thin, brown and graceful.

At our feet we began to notice animal tracks, first one set, then others joining until there was a beaten trail. We followed, and at length found a large hole with water in the bottom of it and tracks coming from all directions. They were the trails of bobcats, once common in all of Florida, now found only in deserted spots, and the destination of their footsteps was a water hole, dug by one or more of them. We hoped to see one, peering down a tree trunk at us, but undoubtedly they saw us first and withdrew. Bobcats are wary of humans, having been mercilessly hunted and nearly exterminated, on account of their occasional fondness for chickens. Their main diet, however, is not chickens but rats, rabbits and other crop-destructive rodents, and they were useful to the very farmers who shot them on sight. They are attractive animals, tawny and spotted, with black-tipped short tails, larger than ordinary cats, about thirty inches long, with short ear tufts. They can be tamed, but even devoted to a human family they remain delightfully wild in their habits. A cat, even a domestic one, is not a creature to be pinned down.

We walked out to the beach, a lonely narrow one. There hurricane and erosion results were most obvious. The sea had taken many of the Australian pines, and their bare gray branches supported cormorants spreading their wings to dry. Life slowed to a stop, and the solitude was absolute, as in a ruined cathedral. The cormorants, motionless on their dark branches over the white beach covered with broken bits of sun-bleached shells, could have been carved long ago and left there. Only the blue restless water moved, eddying around the dead trees, reaching up to undermine the live ones.

We went back along the ravaged beach around the end of the island, where we had beached our boat. Looking across

Uprooted trees on the lonely beach of Upper Captiva support cormorants spreading their wings to dry. Only bobcats live on this eroded island.

the riotous current of Redfish Pass to the large civilized hotel on the other side, the feeling became even stronger that Upper Captiva was what all of Sanibel and Captiva used to be before the Spanish came. The water was a barrier to civilization. It washed the islands apart before there was much development, and the island we stood on stayed as it was, almost untouched, a haunt of rare water birds and animals — deer, panther and bobcat — that can no longer exist on the rest of the Sanibel Island chain.

We stood in a place of peace, where the only strife was the everyday life of nature, and man was one and a half million years away. It was a lonely thought, and a good one, to find oneself back in a time when all the earth was like this.